TRACKING THE STONE MAN

WEST VIRGINIA'S BIGFOOT

SECOND EDITION

DR. RUSSELL JONES

BEYOND THE FRAY

Publishing

BEYOND THE FRAY

Publishing

CONTENTS

PART ONE
HOW BIGFOOT CAME INTO MY LIFE

PART TWO
WHAT WE KNOW AND WHAT WE THINK WE KNOW

PART THREE
WEST VIRGINIA, BIGFOOT'S MOUNTAIN HOME

THE APPENDIXES

In Memory of Jack Jones

To the man who pushed me to be a better man and that I never heard say an unkind word about anyone.
To live a life loved by your family is a good life.
To live a life loved by everyone's family is to have lived an exceptional life.

FORWARD BY MATT MONEYMAKER

Russ Jones is a very credible and reliable Bigfoot investigator who has been checking out reports in and around West Virginia for many years. He has led successful expeditions and is a walking encyclopedia of Bigfoot cases and locations in West Virginia. When producers of the hit television show *Finding Bigfoot* need to go in West Virginia or nearby zones in surrounding states, we speak to him first. Russ has poured all that knowledge into this book. It chronicles his interest and involvement in the subject, starting from his childhood. Russ writes about many places in West Virginia that I have never explored but would like to someday. West Virginia is the Olympic Peninsula of the east in terms of its density of Bigfoots.

Russ isn't done investigating and compiling reports and locations for West Virginia. I predict there will be a second volume of this book someday, which will include reports and locations that are currently being investigated by him and several others.

After working on the TV show *Finding Bigfoot* for five years, I have noticed that people, including government employees, are much more open to the Bigfoot subject. This increased awareness will yield unprecedented evidence in due time.

FORWARD BY MATT MONEYMAKER

January 29, 2016

Matt Moneymaker is the founder and president of the Bigfoot Field Research Organization (BFRO) and host of Finding Bigfoot on the Animal Planet channel.

FOREWORD BY CLIFF BARACKMAN

Stories of Bigfoot encounters from West Virginia have been trickling in to me via my website for a long time. For as long as I've been soliciting eyewitness reports from the public, a respectable number of them have been from the Mountain State, and with a nickname like that, it's no surprise. The entire state lies within the Appalachian Mountain Range, and nearly 80% of its land is forested.

The mountains of West Virginia are craggy, inaccessible, thickly vegetated, and sparsely populated. Food and water are everywhere. The deer population is off the charts. It's the perfect habitat for Sasquatches.

It wasn't until I first visited West Virginia in 2012 that I truly understood how good the habitat is. It was then that *Finding Bigfoot* filmed its first episode in West Virginia, and I finally got a chance to see what all the hubbub was about. We were led to the best locations by the best researcher in the state, Russ Jones. Russ also played a major role in helping the show film its second episode in West Virginia (the first was so good we went back for seconds). The episodes would have many fewer witnesses if it weren't for Russ.

Russ is the kind of person you'd want on your bigfooting team: personable, intelligent, academic, and detail oriented. It is partly his efforts that put West Virginia on the bigfooting map. For years he has been around collecting reports and doing boots-on-the-ground fieldwork.

With the release of this book, Russ is sharing an accumulated knowledge of Sasquatch picked up through years of fieldwork. He discusses field techniques, the effects of television on the public perception of Bigfoot, the validity of the various kinds of "evidence," and more. This book is a bit more thoughtful than most Bigfoot books due to the variety of the subjects covered.

West Virginia is squatchy, possibly the squatchiest place on the East Coast.

September 13, 2015

Cliff Barackman is most widely known for his work on Animal Planet's Finding Bigfoot. Cliff has been a Sasquatch field researcher for more than twenty years, traveling to forty-four of the fifty states, as well as seven foreign countries on five continents. His vast experience with the subject makes him a sought-after Bigfoot expert for media outlets; he has been featured in the Huffington Post, FOX News, Newsweek magazine, and more. While well versed in Bigfooting field techniques and video analysis, his specialty lies in the footprints and their casts, of which he owns the world's second-largest collection. More recently he has opened the successful North American Bigfoot Center in Boring, Oregon. There he shares his vast knowledge. CliffBarackman.com.

Monongahela National Forest in east-central West Virginia. A juvenile
Bigfoot track only 5 ½ inches long. Found off trail in 2013. Photo courtesy of
Randy Mollomo

THE STONE MAN OF APPALACHIA

"Now in the night, the dark walker came gliding in shadow." Beowulf

Bigfoot, or Sasquatch, is ancient history in the Appalachian Mountains. Throughout Appalachia, Native American tribes, including the Cherokee, Delaware, Iroquois, Mingo, Seneca, and Shawnee, long ago, in variations, named the manlike being who lived alongside them.

THE STONE MAN

The Cherokee in the southern Appalachians named the Stone Man "Nun'yunu'wi." To the north, the Ononodagas of the Iroquois nation called the being "Ot-ne-yar-hed," or the Stonish Giant. Other tribes said the being was "He who dressed in stone."

To all Appalachian Indian tribes, the Stone Man had a reputation for three things. He possessed magical powers. He was a trickster who "enjoyed" playing with humans. And, as with many "Big Man" legends in tribes across the continent, the Stone Man was a cannibal, a monster.

To confirm Stone Man as a cannibal is problematic. However, he seems to have served the useful purpose of being the Appalachian "boogey" man for Native American parents of small children. He was the monster who, if they wandered far, might seize them and carry them away to his rocky lair.

For an excellent treatise of Native American legends, go to the Bigfoot Field Researchers Organization (BFRO.net) and on the opening page click "Pre-Columbian and Early American Legends of Bigfoot-like beings."

While I wanted to open the book with this brief treatise on the Stone Man, the most common term for our barefoot friends is "Bigfoot" or "Sasquatch." So, through the remainder of this book, the Stone Man is generally called either one of these names.

Game camera photo in Tucker County, West Virginia. Possible Bigfoot photo.
Courtesy of Matt Rogers

PREFACE

How in the world does one end up being interested in Bigfoot of all things? I have been a successful chiropractor for thirty-one years. A man of science, with degrees to boot! Nonetheless, inevitably events happen in our lives that shape our interests, thoughts, beliefs, and hobbies. Bigfoot is one of those subjects that interest individuals from all across the spectrum. Among my friends doing Bigfoot research are physicians, a fire chief in a large community, a successful engineer, an airline pilot, and a health care administrator.

Some time ago W. Henner Fahrenbach, PhD, told me he didn't envy me writing a Bigfoot book considering the "dearth" of recent evidence. Henner, in the past, was famous in the Bigfoot community, while being an academic, for the study of purported Bigfoot hair. He developed the "type" for the hair as well as a chart estimating Bigfoot weight. Nonetheless, I told him it was something I was compelled to do. I have been interested in the Bigfoot phenomenon for most of my life, and for about the last fifteen years I have actively conducted field research, both on my own and as a BFRO (Bigfoot Field Research Organization) investigator. Also, after studying the Bigfoot phenomenon, I really found convincing evidence out there, but I just didn't like the way it was presented.

In this book I have used my knowledge and experience as a science-educated doctor, certified master naturalist, and outdoorsman, intermingled with information gained from witness interviews to try to put the reader in the middle of prime Bigfoot habitat in West Virginia. The techniques and theories put forth are applicable in all states and forested areas and on both coasts of the United States. I have also set down relevant arguments for and against the existence of Bigfoot and what a creature like that may be.

I have interviewed over one hundred researchers to gather their opinions. While researchers are generally secretive about their best Bigfoot places, they are very giving about contributing their beliefs and research. Some nights I was so excited after talking to a researcher or witness that I would write for hours. While I don't necessarily agree with all their beliefs, they have challenged my beliefs and expanded my thinking.

The approach I have used is to take someone who is either a Bigfoot novice or an experienced researcher, show them how to go into an area that they have never been to, and be able to not only tell if a Bigfoot may reside in the area, but also how to get close to them if they do. I also feature some of the best reports to come out of West Virginia and surrounding areas, and also detail which parts of the state are most suited for a Bigfoot to exist if one is present.

Whether you are a researcher, a *Finding Bigfoot* or *Expedition Bigfoot* fan, or just interested in the topic, I hope to give you a wealth of new information as well as theories to consider and put into practice. You will also find other topics to consider when enjoying the great outdoors.

This is my work, my attempt, my beliefs, and my mistakes where they lie. Put my findings together with what you know and see what you come up with. Expand on my theories. In the end if we all work together, we can find out the truth, as it exists, in regard to Bigfoot.

As you read this, know that this is the second edition of *Tracking the Stone Man*. The first edition was lucky enough to win some awards and sell around five thousand copies. Some of what I theorized is still on point, but other points are dated. I've learned a lot in these past seven years since the first edition. A lot more time in the woods, hundreds of more witnesses, frustrations, affirmation. Travel with me now as I try to keep the Stone Man on its journey.

Dr. Russell L. Jones, January, 2023

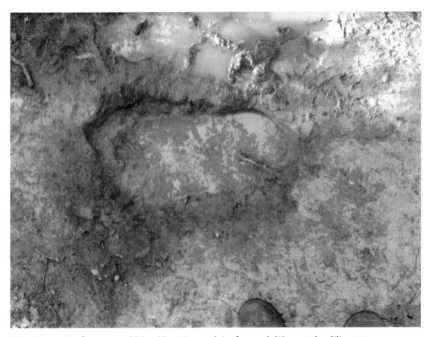

Clay County in the center of West Virginia, track in the mud. We must be diligent to make sure purported tracks are not erosion. Note the depth of the track; this may indicate Bigfoot has a much higher density of body weight per square inch than humans

INTRODUCTION

"All great truths begin blasphemies." George Bernard Shaw

There are many organizations involved in Bigfoot research across the country, the most popular and best known is the Bigfoot Field Research Organization (BFRO). For the past fourteen years I have been a BFRO investigator and expedition organizer. In addition to BFRO groups, most states have a few people who, working either independently or in a group, are actively searching for Bigfoot or Bigfoot evidence. Some groups are very organized; others are loosely bound collections of individuals with varied backgrounds.

The BFRO was founded in 1995 by Matt Moneymaker and has investigators all around the United States and Canada. The investigators are handpicked for the various skills they offer the BFRO and consist of doctors, lawyers, scientists, engineers, biologists, woodsman, and trackers, among other professionals. Yes, a wide variety of individuals who are extremely serious and knowledgeable about what they are doing. So knowledgeable, in fact, that in recent years the BFRO has been featured on Animal Planet's *Finding Bigfoot* television show.

Since I have organized expeditions and have interviewed many witnesses over the years, it seemed only natural that I should take the time to write about the subject. I wanted to give the public the full story from behind the scenes, so to speak. This book's intent is only to let you make up your own mind as to whether it is reasonable to believe that such a thing as Bigfoot could possibly exist.

If there is any state east of the Mississippi that could harbor a secretive, elusive, possibly endangered primate, commonly called Bigfoot, it would be West Virginia. West Virginia nestles among the Appalachian Mountains, one of the oldest mountain ranges in the world, and is the only state found completely within the border of the Appalachian Mountains.

Within West Virginia, 2,500 different species of plants have been identified. West Virginia is a mixed mesophytic forest, one that receives a moderate amount of rainfall. Twenty to twenty-five different tree species compose the majority of the canopy, with none of them dominant. Common trees include oak, beech, hickory, sugar maple, basswood, sumac, tulip poplar, cherry, birch, sour gum, and black walnut. West Virginia is the only state that contains tundra, meaning it has permanently frozen subsoil and supports low-growing vegetations such as lichens. West Virginia also has some of the largest cave systems in the world.

Scientifically, I am going about the search for Bigfoot backwards. Usually one finds an animal, studies it, learns about it, and then writes something. Scientist/author Kenneth Wylie, in his book *Bigfoot, A Personal Inquiry into a Phenomenon*, noted that "Bigfoot writers have forged ahead with elaborate hypothetical concepts anyway, ignoring scientific methodology..." He is right, of course, but I don't see any other way at present.

Traditional scientific means have worked poorly in the past for any number of discoveries, and if Bigfoot exists, traditional methods aren't working now well either. Maybe with all the Bigfoot information now out there, at least the theoretical information, the power of that knowledge, whether completely or only partly correct, will give someone the ability to figure out how to make the discovery.

I want you to go forward with the understanding that in certain circumstances I will not name the exact location in order to protect the witness or preserve a sensitive place. If I tell you a story, it's because I believe it to be true. It could be that I personally know the witness or have experience with those around him or her.

For some sightings, I know of multiple witnesses who do not want to come forward for any number of reasons, such as their job or location, etc. I may have found evidence verifying a witness report. Or, I may have insider knowledge and have confidence in the investigator who studied the report. The flip side of that, of course, is that I do not include in this book reports that I consider unverified or that I have reason to doubt. I am a careful investigator and tend to approach all Bigfoot reports skeptically.

Also, I don't hold myself out to be an expert. I have talked to hundreds of witnesses, spent a lifetime in the woods, read all the books, listened to most all of the podcasts, and interviewed many, many researchers, but still, who can really call themselves a Bigfoot expert? I'm educated on the subject and spend a lot of time in the woods, but that's all I can say about myself. Any mistakes herein are mine. Everything I tell you is as exactly as I recall. If you have a story you want to tell me or think there is an area that I should consider investigating, I would appreciate you reaching out to me at www. TheBigfootDoc.com or DrRLJ@yahoo.com.

Happy hunting!

My ever faithful lab Shade. An awesome athlete in the woods and has a great smeller

PART ONE
HOW BIGFOOT CAME INTO MY LIFE

"The most beautiful thing we can experience is the mysterious."
Albert Einstein

Part 1 is how I became interested in Bigfoot, actually, consumed is a better word, and how it affected my life, beliefs, and investigations. Other researchers' thoughts and opinions have influenced me in many ways. Talking to witnesses, sorting out the facts, and attempting to establish what is really Bigfoot related is fascinating to me. Having Bigfoot in my life has been a worthwhile proposition if for nothing other than the time in the woods and the people I have met. I hope the reader can feel the passion I have for the subject matter.

The author, always in search of remote, isolated beaver dams

CHAPTER 1
EARLY ON

"Some people say that Bigfoot doesn't exist and maybe he doesn't. but all of these people have been seeing something and they can't be making it up."
Vance Winsor in the Clarion News

SOMETHING IN THE WOODS

I first saw tracks on New Year's Day 1977 when I was twelve years old. The day was cold but bluebird sunny. Providentially, New Year's Eve had seen four inches of wet snow. I was hunting rabbits with a friend a little older than me. We had hunted up a hillside that had a hidden cave maybe fifty feet deep. Not many people knew about the cave. The entrance was three-quarters of the way up the hill and hidden by rocks. Unless you walked up the hill and were directly in front of it, you wouldn't even know it was there; you couldn't get to it from above. I had always thought that cave would make a great hidey-hole.

As we climbed the hill, nearing the cave, I saw a fresh track line in the snow. The tracks had just been made. And they looked like human tracks, barefoot, made by someone or something about the size of a normal adult human male. I had the sense that whatever had made them was weathering out the snowstorm in the cave and heard us coming. It left the cave, made fresh tracks, and continued up the hill away from us. It was the 70s, and we thought that maybe someone was on drugs or living in the cave, so I went and looked to see if there was clothes or remnants of a fire, but nothing was in the cave.

A typical Reconyx game camera that the author has over forty in place across West Virginia and southeast Ohio

WE KNEW THE WAY OF THE WOODS

I grew up in an outdoors family living in southeastern Ohio. My family is good salt-of-the-earth people, honest, hardworking, believing a man's word is his measure. And they live in Vinton County, Ohio's most rural county. To this day Vinton County has few traffic lights. Wayne National Forest (the "Wayne" to locals) and Zaleski State Forest cover much of the county, and the majority of the rest of the land is woods and wilderness. When I was growing up, it was uncommon to see a No Trespassing sign.

My family lived outdoors. Not literally, of course, we lived in a house, but while many families liked to hunt, hike, or to be outdoors, to them that meant every now and then. My family was outdoors almost all of the time. We searched for ginseng and wild mushrooms, trapped and fished, and hunted every animal that came in season. We spent so much time in the woods that we believed that nothing lived there that wasn't more afraid of us than we were of it. Ironically, and maybe for that reason, when I had an experience that I couldn't explain, I was never fearful but only curious.

I spent many days and nights in the woods, often with my father, grandfather, and other family members, hunting in remote areas. I would usually take time to point out, to the dismay of my grandfather I'm sure, every track in the woods, wondering what animal made it, and what they were doing. I knew tracking and animal tracks, but I had also learned how we knew what we knew. I not only learned the sign, the spoor, I tried to learn how to "think" like animals thought, how to see the woods as they saw it. Despite this, the footprints coming out of the cave were a mystery to me. Nothing to be afraid of, mind you, simply something unexplained in the woods.

My friend Kevin and I spent a while looking at the tracks, trying to figure out what they were. They looked humanlike, but why would a person be walking barefoot way back in the woods when the weather was so cold? Was the man on drugs? Had a vagrant found the cave and chosen to live there? What kind of man would do something so crazy? I looked inside the cave and couldn't see any indications of anyone living there, no trash or evidence of a fire. We talked about following the tracks but decided to get family to come and look. As we hiked downhill away from the cave, we heard a single, loud, animal-like cry, some kind of yell or noise that we had not heard before. We looked at each other, curious, and moved on.

When we got back to the house, the family was enjoying family holiday time and staying warm on such a cold day. They weren't interested in going out. Actually, it was surprising that none of them had been out hunting, but I guess that was fate, just one of those days. My father and I have talked many times about how our lives may be different had the family gone out and looked at those tracks. As it was, the tracks simply became an odd thing seen in the woods, and they were pushed back in my mind until the next summer.

THE NEXT SUMMER

Sometime in June or July, I went fishing with an uncle. There was a beaver dam about a mile or so back up a hollow that created a pond covering several acres. No trail led to the location. On the main road the creek was, and still is, so small that in places it can be jumped across. As I recall, the family found this fishing hole while coon hunting; no one would ever guess that it was back there. But we knew, and we went there often. I had been to our fishing hole many dozens of times in both daylight and at dark and had never encountered anything unusual. I never saw a track, litter, or any indication that anyone else was ever there. It was just a remote beaver pond, full of large bass, bluegills, and loads of catfish.

My uncle and I were fishing from the beaver dam where it swings close to the hillside on the other bank. The woods on that bank were about thirty-five yards away and very brushy. While quietly fishing, I heard something walking down the hillside. I remember seeing my uncle look up toward the sound. I thought it was a deer, watching us.

When loud screaming started, we knew it wasn't a deer. Something was making very "monkey-like" sounds and screams while at the same time shaking the bushes. We knew this wasn't something that a human could do, especially since we were both wearing pistols. My uncle came close to me. I asked him what it was. With his eyes searching the woods, he said, "Just look for a tree to climb." Whatever it was would have to come across water to get to us. I was shocked but mostly bewildered about what could have been making such noises, but I began looking around on our side for a tree.

Abruptly, as fast as the sounds had started, they stopped. The commotion seemed to last a long time, but it might have only been a minute or so. We had absolutely no idea what it was.

At that time in my life, I had never heard of Bigfoot. The same year I saw the new television series starring Leonard Nimoy *In Search Of*. I'm not sure if I saw a new episode or a rerun, but the episode I saw focused on a mysterious animal some people were calling Bigfoot. I was shocked. I remember wondering if Bigfoot had anything to do with the tracks and the screams I had experienced. As an add-on, decades later I asked my uncle what he believed we had experienced, he smiled and said Bigfoot.

Over the next few years when I was squirrel hunting, I found a single print near a clear-cut. Sometime later, my father and I found a heel print while walking back to fish at the same beaver dam. Interestingly, about the same time (1980), there were media reports from Columbus, Ohio, about two hours north, about a series of Bigfoot sightings barely five miles from the general area I was having these experiences. I recall that around a hundred people came down from Columbus and surrounding areas to invade a particular section of Zaleski State Forest.

Vinton County, Ohio. The cave the author found tracks coming out of and his initial Bigfoot interaction

Years later when I became involved with the Bigfoot Field Research Organization (BFRO), I saw the report about the original incidents in the early 1980s. It was so surreal to be involved in the hunt now while at the same time being in the area of one of Ohio's most well-known Bigfoot encounters while it was taking place. If true, in all likelihood, based on the rarity of the animal, it could have well been the same Bigfoot.

Apparently, some people (a couple of different neighbors) believed they saw a Bigfoot, and a Bigfoot had possibly been shot and wounded.

I remember asking my grandfather what he thought it was, my grandfather probably being the most well-known person in that area and a renowned outdoorsman; he thought it was a bear. However, keep in mind, very few bears roamed Ohio in the 1970s; even now the resident bear population hovers between fifty and a hundred resident bears.

LIFE IN WEST VIRGINIA

About then it was college time for me, so I went out of the state, first four years in Indiana for undergraduate, and then another four or five in Iowa. After finishing my doctoral degree, I moved to West Virginia. It appealed to me to be able to buy hundreds of acres teeming with wildlife and live only ten minutes or so from the state capital. I mean, in how many states can you do that? I still hunted and hiked some, but most of my energy went into building a big practice. I had little time for searching for a mysterious animal in the wilderness that now surrounded me.

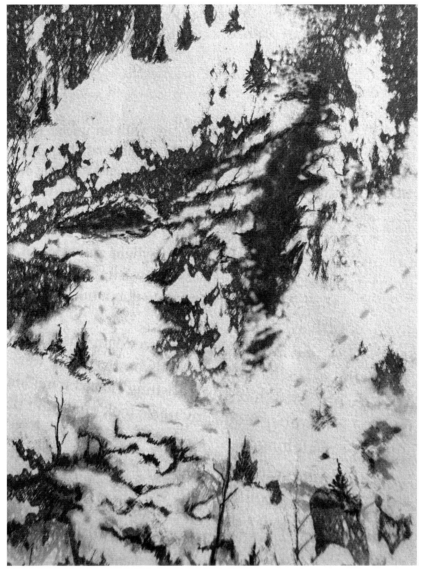

"Tracks in the Snow." Illustration by Sybilla Irwin representing the first tracks the author saw

CHAPTER 2
BIGFOOT REVISITED

"Being a believer is great, finding out on your own is better." Marc DeWerth, Bigfoot researcher, speaker, and director of the world's largest Bigfoot conference.

SERIOUS ABOUT BIGFOOT YET AGAIN

As the years went by and my practice got squared away, I found even more time to spend outdoors and again began to think actively about Bigfoot. I attended a fantastic year-long master naturalist program sponsored by the state of West Virginia, which introduced me to things I hadn't even considered in the past.

I began to understand and think about the effects of altitude, foods available in different areas, how the flora and fauna are related to their environment, and how it was possible for certain animals to exist in certain areas. All aspects of a forest ecosystem are balanced, and every element needs to be right in order for animals of certain types to exist in certain areas. The idea of Bigfoot as an unknown primate, nothing more, nothing less, came to be the only rational explanation for our unusual experiences in the hills.

During all that time, I read anything I could find on the internet and literally any book I could find out there on the subject of Bigfoot. In that spirit, I want to first summarize some reasonable, rational, concrete information we have about Bigfoot.

Vinton County, Ohio. Where the bushes were shaken and the author was screamed at by an unknown creature. Water used to be at the top of the bank

Also called Sasquatch, Yahoo, and many hundreds of other names, Bigfoot is an upright bipedal primate covered in hair. According to many reports, Bigfoot hair is reddish-brown, but may also be shades of brown, black and gray. Such variation in coloring is common in nature, and in fact, the differing reports of Bigfoot's coloring are similar to the fur color and variations seen in coyotes, another animal known to range widely and adapt to many different niches.

Friends who study possible Bigfoot hair have told me that, regardless of the general color of a Bigfoot hair, under a powerful microscope there is always at least a slight reddish tinge or hint of red in Bigfoot hair. Bigfoot's hair covers most of the body except the palm of the hands, soles of the feet, and some of the face. Bigfoot is an omnivore, eating both plants and animals. It is rare, curious, and generally wary of humans. Bigfoot spend the majority of their time in solitary locations.

Thought to exist as individuals or in small family groups, Bigfoot has a history going back thousands of years in North America, while being acknowledged by Indians for hundreds of years, and in print for roughly 150 years. It may have relatives across the globe that are similar and have their own name in local legend: Yeti, Yeren, Yowie, Almasty, and many others. Whether or not Bigfoot's relatives across the globe exist, I can't say, and if they do, I have no idea if they are the same species that we have in North America. I am strictly concentrating on the animal said to exist in North America.

Bigfoot are believed to communicate through vocalizations and possibly by the structures of trees, sticks made into glyphs, and rock arrangements in their habitat, which is primarily remote, isolated woodlands. However, Bigfoot can be found in almost any area that provides water, food, and security. Sightings have come from all states except Hawaii, with the most reports coming from the Pacific Northwest. Although the evidence of Bigfoot's existence is compelling, it is not yet enough to satisfy science.

So, I learned the basic facts, as we believe we understand them, about Bigfoot; and somewhere along the way I saw that the annual Ohio Bigfoot Conference, then run by Don Keating, was coming up. Dr. Jeff Meldrum was scheduled to speak. The conference was being held only two hours away at Salt Fork State Park in Ohio. I had read Dr. Meldrum's book *Legend Meets Science* and wanted to meet him in person, so I decided to attend. Dr. Meldrum, while not the first scientist to investigate and publicly talk about Bigfoot, was certainly the most popular at the time. He continues to be a very prominent and popular authority on the subject.

BIGFOOT PEOPLE UP CLOSE AND PERSONAL

When I went to my first Bigfoot event, I never imagined that I would one day research Bigfoot, much less lead expeditions for the public, and become an investigator doing television, radio, and internet shows on the subject. I was just interested, consumed, passionate about

Bigfoot. All going back to my experiences when I was younger, I just needed to know, to understand. Now I realize that I was like a dog on a bone, I just couldn't let go. Having spent so much time in the woods, I instinctually knew that I had experienced something out of the ordinary.

I've met so many great friends and mentors through the years in Bigfoot. As Cliff Barackman says, "Bigfoot is the one fields of study in which your inspirations can become your friends"

The Ohio Bigfoot Conference was my first exposure to the Bigfoot culture (a subject that is a whole book in itself). Under the careful stewardship of Don Keating, the conference had been going on for many years, with steadily increasing numbers. Keating is a legend in Ohio bigfooting. I believe around three hundred people attended the conference that year, but I didn't know a soul. I sat in the middle of strangers and listened to them present various theories and beliefs regarding an animal that almost everyone there believed existed. I was surprised that their descriptions of the creatures seemed to be almost as various as the attendees.

Bigfoot culture and politics are interesting. Certain groups won't talk to other groups: There are people I will call naturalists or flesh and blood people, people like myself who believe Bigfoot is an "as yet" unrecognized primate; ghost hunters who believe Bigfoot is essentially a ghost phenomenon; paranormalists, whose beliefs are often referred to by others as "woo"; and the alien and Bigfoot crowd who believe Bigfoot is either an alien or that there is some relationship between Bigfoot and UFOs per the Star Wars paradigm.

Then there are the "kill" versus "no-kill" partisans who continually debate the practical and moral ramifications of trying to produce a body to settle the Bigfoot question once and for all. Unfortunately, these people "converse" at an otherworldly level as they don't seem to realize that people with purpose can't even get a long enough look at Bigfoot to even take a picture.

At my first conference an older woman asked a witness what color shirt he was wearing when the encounter happened. He answered, and she nodded as if that explained everything! I had no idea what she was talking about, still don't. The whole conference was confusing, but fascinating.

As I said, I belong to the naturalist or flesh and blood group of Bigfoot hunters. In many ways, we part from the other types, listening but usually skeptical of their debates. We are science-minded individuals who compose maybe 10 or 15% of the community. We don't care about the fluff and are strictly interested in the meat of the matter, what can be observed, measured, and collected.

Even for a naturalist type I am particularly hardheaded. I want there to be no doubt about the evidence presented. I think in general that fluff and pseudoscience make it difficult for interested scientists to become involved, and I can see why; quite frankly, it's just too risky for them professionally until a specimen is discovered.

While talking to a friend on the drive home after the first conference, she asked my thoughts on the conference. I didn't want to insult anyone, so I said, "Well, there were some interesting people there."

"I don't want to be mean," she said, "but you were at a Bigfoot conference."

I got what she was talking about. Belief in Bigfoot is unusual to begin with, so I hope this book will demonstrate not all Bigfoot believers are guided by an inner compulsion. I hope to show there are open-minded researchers and naturalists who cannot reconcile soundly documented incidents with current scientific knowledge, which leads me and others to believe that Bigfoot does exist.

The Ohio Bigfoot Conference is now larger than ever and run by my friend Marc DeWerth. Marc himself is a wealth of Bigfoot knowledge and can tell you something about almost every Bigfoot report in Ohio. He has traveled to almost every area of the state. Ironically, considering how few people I knew in the Bigfoot community, years later I was asked back to the conference as a speaker a few times. Apparently, organizers believed I brought something worthy to the conversation. I went from not knowing anyone in the Bigfoot world to speaking at the largest conference several years later. I really threw myself into the subject and have ever since.

Pocahontas County, West Virginia. The Cranberry Wilderness Area. The largest wilderness area in the eastern United States

And now I believe that, in fact, West Virginia with its miles of uninhabited, mountain forests hosts a population of Bigfoot that could number in the hundreds.

BECOMING A BIGFOOT INVESTIGATOR

After my interest was piqued by the conference, I found the BFRO.net website and immersed myself in their database. This database lists thousands of sightings across the country that have been analyzed by one of the BFRO investigators. On the front page of the website I noticed that they were soon to host one of their public expeditions. "What the heck!" I thought. "The worst that can happen is that they are weird, and I will go home!"

If you have never been to one of these expeditions and are interested in Bigfoot, you should try it. Potential participants are interviewed, pay a fee, and sign a waiver and a nondisclosure agreement. Then the fun begins! My first expedition was led by Mark Maisel, one of the first investigators in the BFRO. But I got even luckier; Matt Moneymaker, the founder of the group, was also present! With the popularity of the *Finding Bigfoot* television show, it's now rare for Matt to be able to be on these expeditions. Like investigators for the group, people who go on the expeditions represent a wide and varied segment of our population. I found a group of people of whom about half had had experiences like mine, and the other half were just interested in Bigfoot.

If you think a whole weekend of talking about Bigfoot sounds boring, an expedition is probably not for you. A lot of people have trouble imagining a group of people who literally talk all day and deep into the night about Bigfoot, but really, that is what happens. Going to expeditions is usually how you get approached to be an investigator. If you get along with the investigators and have a solid background and outdoor experience, you may be invited to join the BFRO. Thanks to Matt and Mark, I was invited! After some careful training by the group's secretary, Caroline Curtis, I began investigating reports in Ohio and West Virginia for the group.

Still a man of science and always looking for the most likely natural cause of an incident in the woods, I started interviewing witnesses, always keeping my "skepticals" on, as the late Ray Crowe of the Western Bigfoot Society used to say. At the point I started doing this, I thought that there was a chance that there was something out there. I also believed that it was most likely in the Pacific Northwest if it did exist. I knew that I personally had some unusual things happen to me in the woods of southeastern Ohio but couldn't definitively say it was a Bigfoot.

Usually, people are invited to be investigators if there aren't enough investigators in a particular state or if you bring unique talents to the group. It used to be only the founder, Matt Moneymaker, would make the invitations. He primarily chose people he thought would best benefit the group. Matt had a certain vision of what he was after, and it has worked well for two decades. With the success Matt has had with television and other commitments, while still holding the steering wheel of the group, others needed to step up and help out, and fortunately they have.

Usually, investigators are chosen out of an expedition dependent upon what value a group of investigators place on what you have to offer in whatever capacity it may be. We have scientists, doctors, lawyers, firefighters, police officers, tech people, people good with witnesses, outdoorsmen—a really wide variety of individuals in order to capture a broad group of perspectives. We even have a talented artist named Sybilla Irwin who helps our witnesses create sketches of what the Bigfoot in a particular sighting looked like.

Most often you go on a number of expeditions before the group decides whether you are a good fit personality-wise, which is really important because we spend so much time together and have to spend long hours sometimes deep in the wilderness in the total darkness with no help around for miles.

Once you are asked to participate, you get trained to talk to witnesses, evaluate reports, and how to actually do the reports. If we feel that the report is good enough, then we publish it on the BFRO website. The percentage of submitted reports suitable for publishing is small. I estimate about one out of fifty reports I handle is published by the BFRO website. I want to make sure only the most reliable and compelling sightings are published. At any one time I am probably handling twenty active cases. Active meaning that they have been sent to me, one way or another, and I am exchanging emails, phone calls, or arranging a meeting with the witness, and have not yet reached a conclusion about submitting a case.

Being an investigator is a labor of love, and all of us across North America take it very seriously. None of us are doing it for a living. We do it because we believe in the group and the cause. We all have jobs and are doing the investigations and reports in our free time. We do something Bigfoot related almost every day. We are Bigfoot geeks.

We talk to witnesses each week. I am on the internet three to four times a day, checking to see if there are any new reports in my region. I don't want to take a chance on something that might have just happened. For instance, a few years ago, I visited a teacher who sighted a Bigfoot running through a freshly plowed garden. I was able to get there to look at the track just hours after the sighting.

As I was writing this, a report came in from a coon hunter in a location I had been at just two days prior. Something could break at any time!

There is a sense of comradery and team among the investigators. We talk often and listen to each other's reports to help evaluate possible evidence. We usually go to at least a few private expeditions a year that are for investigators only. The purpose is to evaluate a location for an expedition or spend time in a sensitive location that may or may not be on private property. We also usually go to a couple of public expeditions to help the investigator in charge with whatever help we can give to him or her.

We develop deep relationships that extend beyond Bigfoot, and some of our closest friends are in the group. When we get together, we spend literally hours and hours debating Bigfoot-related topics and catching up with all of our own investigations. Nationally, we communicate daily with each other via a private email group. We discuss new information that may be possible evidence; we discuss evidence in the attempt to reach a consensus on our beliefs, and bounce things off another who is respected in the Bigfoot community.

LEADING AN EXPEDITION

When you have been in the group long enough and are deemed able, you may be asked to organize an expedition. This is really a labor of love. Not only do you have to pick a location that has had, and hopefully will have, Bigfoot activity, the location also must be able to accommodate a group, which may number twenty-five to fifty people.

At the Large conferences investigators from all over the world come together to share theories and stories. Lots of one on one time with friend investigators sharing secrets

I did an Ohio expedition one year and partnered up with investigator Darren Pevarnik to do a couple in West Virginia. You have to personally call and interview each person applying, and that takes hours and hours to accomplish. Darren and I probably made three or four road trips to different locations to look around for a couple of days each. Then you spend about a week on location when your expedition is taking place.

During the day we like to have classes, which might include track-

ing, casting of tracks, audio instruction and interpretation, prepared-
ness, thermal education, habituation cases, and many more topics.
Also during the day, we may point out several promising locations or
locations of previous sightings for participants to explore. We are
usually in a scenic area, which makes exploration even more enjoyable.

Next, we take the people out at night and try to have great technology for them to use. During the night walks, we set them up in
small groups with experienced investigators to learn about Bigfoot and
the woods at night.

Participants arrive on Thursday and leave on Sunday morning.
Organizing investigators work hard to make sure there is a wide
variety of participants. The backgrounds of the participants are as wide
and varied as the investigators. Doctors to students come to experience
a weekend of fun.

As the organizer, you always sweat getting Bigfoot activity. I have
been out on a few expeditions when it rained torrentially, and nothing
in the woods moved, including Bigfoot. One time when we were out,
we ran into a group of Rainbow People, counterculture types who
meet in America's national forests. Coon hunters' dogs can be an issue.
Bear hunters and their dogs are commonly running about the mountains year-round. In general we try to avoid deer, bear, and turkey
hunting seasons when scheduling an expedition. The organizer picks a
good location based on history and one he or she thinks will be a likely
place for a Bigfoot encounter. But, as we say, in the end, the Bigfoot
must want to "come out and play."

It's funny how little time most people spend outdoors. At night,
seldom is anyone outside in the forests of the country. I have seen the
most muscled of men become very afraid at night in the woods. We
always have small groups and experienced people with each group,
but just being out there at night, if one is not used to it, can be a new
and terrifying thing! Even familiar woods and trails look completely
different at night. The sounds at night are unfamiliar and completely
different than during the day.

One night one of my investigator friends, Brad Kennan, was
leading a group when a man in the group said, "I hear something! It's
right over there!" Brad said, "Yeah, it's a mouse. I'm watching it on the

thermal." The man said, "No way! It's something very big!" Brad said again, "It's a mouse." Brad heard a large scuffle and banging and turned on his light to see the large muscular man bracing for an impact of something large coming from the woods! That's the way it goes. The man was gone the next day.

The woods are very quiet at night, and a lot of birds and animals make strange sounds as well. In fact, it's very common for participants to disappear after the first night in the woods. They find that they just don't like being in the woods at night and leave for home. Many times it seems like the people who like scary movies are the ones who are the most fearful in the woods at night. Being cold or wet in the woods isn't pleasant; add scared to that and it can be a deal breaker.

For instance, owls can make both wondrous and horrible sounds at night. If you didn't know all the sounds that the owl can make, you might swear on hearing one, there were monkeys in the woods. I remember one night I was driving with investigators Pevarnik and Maisel when we pulled back into a remote dead-end hollow in the middle of the night. As soon as we turned the vehicle off, we heard a "whoop!" Excited, we got out and set chairs up to listen for a while. After about thirty minutes of silence and starting to nod off, we were scared to death by the screech and roar (I use the term loosely) of an owl right over our heads! There is something not quite right about an animal that scares people at night.

Another time I walked a group back a couple of miles into a wilderness area. The group included two "city girls" from Cleveland, Ohio. Both were nice and kind, but with little or no outdoor and nighttime experience. When we got settled in, I asked everyone to turn off their red lights and let their night vision adjust. On cloudy nights deep in the woods, it is dark, darker than some people have ever witnessed. Just as soon as our lights went out, an owl that was close by let out a horrible sound! One of the girls from Cleveland shrieked, "What in the hell was that?!"

One of many interesting lectures at a BFRO expedition

I know that there can be a perception in the Bigfoot community that investigators are making a lot of money doing the expeditions, but they really are a labor of love. The amount of money we receive from an expedition is just enough to pay for the food we provide partici-pants, all the phone calls, emails, weeks in the field for preparation, the cost of gas, and taxes. That said, I'm sure some investigators make a little money on their expeditions; everyone in the public hopes to be paid for their time. But I'm sure the income, calculated on an hourly basis, is very meager. I like being in the BFRO and want to do my part for the cause. I make no money from the expeditions I have organized; quite frankly, I lose money every time.

MY WILD PASSION

All this said, I want to add a few observations before I get into the meat of this book. First, I want to mention that I get all kinds of reac-tions when people discover my interest in Bigfoot. Some simply give me a type of knowing smile. Others are extremely interested. On balance, I have found most people to be respectful of my pursuit of the truth.

Has Bigfoot investigation hurt my reputation as a doctor, professional, and master naturalist? I'm really not sure. I have gotten to the point that it's bigger than me, and I want to know the truth, all of the truth. I sense that if most people knew all that I have experienced, they might be equally enthralled. I am hoping that, as you read this book, you will become as fascinated as I am.

Possible Bigfoot track found by investigator Brad Kennan. Dr. Jeff Meldrum noted that it definitely was not a bear and the animal was apparently shifting back and forth

Will it change my life when Bigfoot is acknowledged to be real? Will I call everyone and say, "I told you so"? I might briefly do that, but I'm not that sort of man. If the acknowledgment doesn't happen in my lifetime, will I feel as if I have wasted my time? No. I will never regret the hours spent in the woods in some of the most beautiful places that exist. I only hope that I am blessed with good health in my later life so I can spend all the time that I innately crave to finding the little treasures in the woods and, possibly, a huge treasure.

A purported Bigfoot track

PART TWO
WHAT WE KNOW AND WHAT WE THINK WE KNOW

"Given the scientific evidence I have examined, I'm convinced there's a creature out there that is yet to be identified." Dr. Jeff Meldrum, Professor of Anatomy and Anthropology at Idaho State University.

This part is a summary of arguments for and against the existence of Bigfoot combined with my perspective on the subject. My perspective comes from decades of reading Bigfoot literature, studying the different hominid lineage possibilities, and my science and medical education. I believe the chapters in this part summarize my thoughts in a most positive and concise manner.

As I mentioned, this part has taken decades of study, thought, outlining, writing, and revision. In just the last ten years I would guess we have seen a twofold increase in researchers switching their Bigfoot origin beliefs from ape to *Homo* line. I now commonly hear researchers say "primate" in the hope of covering all possibilities of how Bigfoot may have actually evolved. Lastly, keep in mind that what we learn in the future may change some of my beliefs, but more importantly, may cause revisions to science. Enjoy

"Dad and I find a track." My father and I found another track a couple of months after the author was screamed at. Illustration by Sybilla Irwin

CHAPTER 3
BIGFOOT LIVES

"I don't ever call myself a believer, it's not a belief. I'm absolutely convinced that Sasquatch exists." Dr. Grover Krantz, author and anthropologist at Washington State University

WHY PEOPLE SAY THERE IS NO BIGFOOT, AND WHY THEY ARE WRONG

Many people claim that Bigfoot doesn't exist, and some even argue that Bigfoot couldn't possibly exist. Sometimes these claims are made from a simple refusal to believe what has not been scientifically documented. Such claims essentially say, "If it was out there, we would know it. We don't know it, so it can't be out there."

This, of course, is nonsense. New species are discovered at a rate of around fifteen thousand every year. While most are small, some are fairly large. Just a few years ago, we first documented the presence of Isabel's saki (*Pithecia isabela*), a monkey in Peru. In addition, about 150 years ago, mountain gorillas were merely a rumor as far as science was concerned (first referred to in print in 1847 as troglodytes because they were thought to live in caves). No proof existed until natives produced a body, not scientists, natives. Similarly, the giant panda existed only as folklore and anecdotal evidence in rural China until the early twentieth century.

There are a variety of more tangible reasons people refuse to belief in the existence of an unidentified primate lurking in the woods, or frankly even consider it. Most of them come down to three main claims.

1. There is not enough food to support such an animal.

Some say, "An adult animal like a Bigfoot would require an immense amount of calories, and there isn't enough out there to eat." So the argument goes. Most of those who make the argument are laypeople who know little or nothing about caloric requirements or carrying capacities of the environment. They have no idea if enough food exists. I haven't heard any naturalist or other professional make the same argument. It's common knowledge among those who have that type of training that there is plenty of food. But just to cover this argument, let me make a few comments about it.

Bears are similar in size and do not have the analytical thinking skills of primates. Bears have little problem getting enough food. They commonly hibernate a few months in the winter, but they eat way more food than normal in the months before hibernation in order to prepare for their long "naps." If bears can make it in warm months, then Bigfoot can as well; they just have to get through the winter months, and any animal smart enough to exist undiscovered is clever enough to get through winters.

The first thing I would do if I were a Bigfoot in cold weather would be to move to a lower elevation. I'm sure that caves, rock overhangs, and old mines are used by many species in times of storms or extreme weather. In my chiropractic practice, I have treated someone who works with the Abandoned Mine Program in West Virginia. He told me that such mines number in the thousands, and if family mines are included, probably tens of thousands. Or perhaps, like coyotes, during the winter, Bigfoot just stay outside.

As for the availability of food: mushrooms, honeysuckle, cattails, ramps, wild onions, berries, pine nuts, dandelions, pokeweed, roots spruce tips, and highland plantain are available all year long. As are deer, birds, rabbits, raccoons, possums, mice, housecats, roadkill, refuse, crop gleanings, and silage. This is by no means a complete list; there are hundreds of foods available all year. West Virginia's winter landscape might look barren to most of us, but not to the many wild animals that are definitely out there through the winter.

Typical gated gas well or old timber road that lead to deep and isolated forests. These are located all over Appalachia

A large omnivorous primate is going to choose foods dense in nutrients and calories. Out west, large herbivores weighing many hundreds of pounds, such as moose and elk, are able to get through much harsher winters than those found in the Appalachian Mountains. A large component of their upbringing as a juvenile Bigfoot probably involves learning to find food sources in the winter, and Bigfoot, as a primate, is probably better adapted to learning than a moose or elk.

2. The body of a Bigfoot has never been found.

A natural resources biologist who works in West Virginia once pointed out to me that no one has ever found a bear in the wild that had died of natural causes. There are lots and lots of bears roaming around, so it seems only natural that a few dead bears would be found, but no. Maybe a dying Bigfoot, like an old dog or sick cat, simply crawls off to some remote place when it knows its time is coming.

Many of the places frequented by Bigfoot, like West Virginia, have very acidic soils that leave few bones or fossils. What bones are left are eaten by mice, squirrels, or other critters largely for their mineral content. Regardless of the time of year, scavengers ravage and spread the remains, even faster in the winter than in the summer. Many documentaries document this. On YouTube there are amazing videos showing how quickly nature reclaims animals that have died.

It's unlikely that bones in nature exist longer than a year. Teeth and antlers are harder and can last longer, but it's difficult to find even random bones scattered in the wilderness. And quite frankly, I don't know of anyone in West Virginia who is searching for bones. It's most common to come upon animal bones from deer or other smaller prey animals. Rarely are the bones of a predator found, especially animals like wolves or wolverines, which have low population numbers.

It has been theorized that Bigfoot bury their dead; perhaps they do. Elephants and apes are known to heap things on top of their dead, so maybe Bigfoot does something like that. It's a possibility. Whether Bigfoot conceal their dead by burying or covering, or simply leave them out in the open, there are so few that it's unlikely anyone will stumble across a dead Bigfoot. Author Chris Murphy once told me that "Bones are so few and rare that it is more likely to find a Bigfoot than its bones." Few people are out in the woods, and even fewer roam the remote wildernesses. You have to have people out there in order to find anything.

Lastly, who's to say Bigfoot bones haven't been found? I'm sure people have walked over many bones in the woods concealed by forest debris. Few people would bother to pick up a bone unless it was so large you couldn't help but notice it—especially if it looked like a large human skull. The skull bones are the hardest in the body and the most likely to be found intact. So even when bones are found, they might not be identified because of being broken, decomposed, or other reasons.

Throughout history many bones that were extremely large or looked different for one reason or another have been turned over to museums. The American Museum of Natural History and the Smithsonian have tens of millions of specimens and not enough resources to go through everything that they have. Loren Coleman, in his book *True Giants*, gives several examples of doctors and universities that at one time had large skulls and bones in their collections only to later have misplaced them, never to locate them again.

If you find enormous trees like this it's apparent that you are most likely in a varied ecosystem. Some of the old trees were in inaccessible areas that were hard to get horses to when timbering

3. There isn't enough unpopulated or untraveled land for Bigfoot to remain hidden.

West Virginians have a keen awareness of how much untamed land surrounds them, but it's hard when one lives in a large city to comprehend the vastness of America's forests. These city dwellers are living their busy lives, working and playing; Bigfoot is not really a consideration. They think about the community where they live and occasionally may wonder if something like Bigfoot may exist. Most realize that there are many places that are inhospitable, uninhabited, uninhabitable, and inaccessible. But those same people seldom visit forests, let alone wilderness areas. These are places that take an effort to get to in many states.

Do you know that according to the West Virginia Division of Forestry, seventy-eight (78) percent of the state has forest canopy? Thirty-six (36) percent of the United States is forested. While in decline in much of the world, there is more forest in the United States than there was just one hundred years ago.

I don't think that most people know or care. If an animal like a Bigfoot needs roughly five hundred square miles (I don't think it's that much) that has inaccessibility and resources to exist, like those in a rain forest, West Virginia has that many times over. You can easily check this for yourself by using Google Earth or a like program for a look. It's really shocking how much remote and inaccessible land there is throughout West Virginia. The steepness of the land can't be appreciated by anything other than a visit. I always try to take a picture to give people an idea, and it just doesn't do it justice.

Despite these objections, I became convinced of Bigfoot's existence for a lot of different reasons, as have many other people. About a third of the nation's population believes something like Bigfoot may exist. Perhaps the most famous primatologist of the last hundred years, Jane Goodall, also believes. In an interview on NPR she stated that she was "sure they exist." Goodall is known for her exhaustive experience living with and observing chimpanzees in the wild.

Track over 14 inches long found in early spring. This is an excellent example of the mid-tarsal break in a Bigfoot track. Notice the heel imprint, the rise from the mid-tarsal break and the rolling motion of the front part of the foot

CHAPTER 4
ELEMENTS OF BELIEF

"This could be a case where biology and mythology correspond." Dr. Robert Michael Pyle, lepidopterist and author

WHY I BELIEVE WHAT I BELIEVE

I deal with people for a living, hundreds of them a week, for over thirty years.

That is the number one reason that I believe Bigfoot exists. After spending years at my job (31), I think I have a very good feel for people and personalities. Very quickly I can recognize whether someone is being truthful or not, which is malingering in medical terms, or hoaxing in the Bigfoot community. When reviewing my records for the book, I found that I had interviewed so many people that I couldn't even remember them all.

If not for my notes, I wouldn't have believed there had been that many. Most witnesses I have interviewed thought that they were telling the truth. They believed that they saw something. Many times they saw it very close and in daylight. Policemen, teachers, sheriffs, mayors, city council members, hunters, veterans, firefighters, nurses, loggers, doctors, engineers, people with a long outdoor history and many more who were never outdoors. The Bigfoot witnesses are geographic not a demographic. What they have in common is that they all live in an area where Bigfoot exists.

What did they have to gain by sharing their story and many times asking me not to share their name? Many have signed affidavits and passed polygraph tests. Many of the details that they provided regarding the animal's features are strikingly similar and in some instances not well known to the general public or internet. Many times if we (the investigators) are not sure or have some question, we bring in another investigator (or five!) to review the evidence or reinterview the witness. If it is actual physical evidence, we as a group will privately review it. We look at different types of evidence each week, and sometimes they are hotly debated.

Another point that I want to raise about eyewitness accounts, most lawyers, judges, and police officers will tell you that eyewitness account is the least trustworthy of all evidence. I've found that in regard to many things, humans' memory or account is not good. People aren't good at guessing height, weight, or distance for sure. The standard in many legal cases must be higher than in cases such as identification of an animal. While a human witness may not be good at guessing the height of something, surely most are capable of telling whether something is a human or something else. For people living in bear country, it's laughable to think that they can't tell the difference between a bear, which has short legs, a snout, and can walk on two legs a short distance, and something humanlike with long arms, a relatively flat face, and ambulates on two legs quickly.

Each year I take dozens and dozens of reports. Many are misidentifications or just a sound that someone heard. Each year or two I will get an exceptional report such as a park ranger sighting close and in daylight, and frankly, investigators live for the great reports. In rough estimation there are around sixty thousand Bigfoot reports, and it's estimated that only one out of twenty encounters get reported. If one were to throw out all the average reports and just kept the very best, the exceptional, the cream of the crop, say the top couple of hundred, we would be left with such clear accounts with the very best witnesses that it would be clear they were either liars or the account was real.

Given all this, it seems some weight should be attached to witness testimony going back centuries.

THE PATTERSON-GIMLIN FILM

This film, taken by Roger Patterson in northwest California in late October 1967, begins when he was on horseback. The subject is a female Bigfoot, breasts apparent, walking across a sandbar to the forest beyond. At one point, "Patty," as she came to be called, looks back over her shoulder as she walks. The single frame of film of "Patty" turning to look at Roger is probably one of the most viewed and iconic images in film history. And undoubtedly in its whole, the Patterson-Gimlin film remains the single best piece of video evidence that Bigfoot exists.

There are many reproductions of the Patterson-Gimlin footage online, so you have probably seen a segment of the film. There are now stabilized images on YouTube and many analyses there, like the one from National Geographic.

In terms of convincing film footage, I should also mention the Paul Freeman footage, with the acknowledgment that much of Freeman's work has become controversial. Personally, I find it compelling. I had the honor of being a contributing editor of Paul Freeman's son Michael's book *Freeman Bigfoot files*. After having the opportunity to see the never before pictures and interviews I now believe the evidence to be authentic. Much of the previously cited criticisms have now been answered. Some will never be happy with any evidence beyond a body. Both can be seen at BFRO.net along with other credible evidence.

If you google "Bigfoot pictures" or go on YouTube and do the same, you can see literally hundreds of images that people claim to be Bigfoot. Many of these clips or pictures are good and maybe even clearer than the PG film, but with today's video technology, there is just no way to say if they are real or not.

As an example of the murkiness surrounding all the posted clips, I want to mention the recordings made by my friend Bart Cutino of California. His work falls under the video category of thermal footage. Essentially, he captures, with an infrared camera, "heat pictures" made by animals moving in the forest at night. Bart has some great thermal footage of an apparent Bigfoot. If you know him, or one of the friends in this group, you would have no doubt we are telling the truth and what was captured was real. However, the public and the professors, both sitting in their chairs, don't know us and could well and do question the evidence. Frankly, they don't care enough to even investigate the evidence.

In 2014 former Hollywood makeup artist William Munns wrote an extensive and exhaustive book of the Patterson-Gimlin film called *When Roger met Patty*, which you can investigate at whenrogermetpatty.com. If you are interested in the subject, reading the book will leave you with little doubt about the authenticity of the book. Interestingly, since I first wrote this book, podcasts became available with their reams of content. I enjoyed the podcast *Astonishing Legends*' seven-part series on the PG film. Regardless of your stance, it seems reasonable to educate yourself before giving an opinion. I realize in the times of the internet that that's not always the case, sadly.

After the Patterson-Gimlin film was shot, an investigator went to Walt Disney, as they were the best costume makers at the time. The Disney people said they couldn't make the costume; it was impossible with the techniques at the time.

First in 2013, and a few times since, I've had a meal with Bob Gimlin at the Ohio Bigfoot Conference. Over the hours I was able to ask as many questions as I wanted. One thing he told me that had not been reported at that time was, was when Patty looked back in the famous frame 352, she was responding to the splashing made by Gimlin's horse as he crossed the creek.

I have found Mr. Gimlin believable, sincere, and of the utmost character. He continues to maintain the veracity of the film. I'd like to note that Bob Gimlin told me "he never made any money from the film but got plenty of grief."

In the end if the Patterson-Gimlin film was found to be a fake somehow when it hasn't over the last fifty odd years, it doesn't somehow disprove the existence of Bigfoot. It's just another small piece of the ever-growing vault of evidence that is being added to slowly each year.

Bob Gimlin and Dr. Russ Jones at the Ohio Bigfoot Conference

THE TRACKS

Thousands of purported Bigfoot tracks have been found around the United States. Scientists who specialize in primate anatomy and/or Bigfoot anatomy have studied the casts pulled from them. Interestingly, some of the tracks appear to show dermal ridges, which are like fingerprints on the feet.

Verified by fingerprint experts, dermal ridges found on the Bigfoot tracks have linear patterns found on no other identified primate or animal, making them truly unique. I also think one of the most impressive things on these casts are obviously visible sweat pores.

Some of these prints have been found in the most inhospitable and remote locations. A very good photograph of a Bigfoot track was taken in 1947, before modern stories actively began. The earliest cast of a track that I am aware of was made in 1941 by a law enforcement officer in British Columbia, also before the modern era of Bigfoot, so to speak.

One of the features that one learns to look for in track prints is the difference between impressions and ridges. The edge of the footprint, between the foot and the surrounding dirt, offers a clear way to differentiate a real footprint from a fake one.

A real footprint will leave a curved edge. A fake footprint, pressed into the dirt with a foot made of wood, metal, or plastic, will generally have straight edges and ninety-degree angles. In other words, fake footprints leave sharp edges, which are easily detected by seasoned trackers. The ridges left by fake footprints may include cracks in the ground, whereas the anatomical rolling motion of a natural foot will not cause these.

It's also important to look for indications of individual or dynamic toe movement as well as push-off ridges behind the toe. Finally, often in a real Bigfoot track, there will be evidence of the two-part foot as seen in several of the track photographs in this book.

Another point to consider when deciding if tracks or casts are genuine is where does the track fall on the "bell-shaped curve"? This is a math and science term related to statistical probability. Various track information is plotted on a graph. When individual graphs are over-laid, in a "computer stack," so to speak, the closer the individual track characteristics are to the median of a group of other tracks, the greater the probability that the track is real.

If a track has characteristics very different from the "norm," then the probability of the track being genuine is reduced. But the track with the smallest mathematical probability of being real may be a "real, genuine Bigfoot track." It just means we do not have other examples, or enough data, in the database.

Interestingly, reports of tracks come only from areas with at least twenty inches of precipitation annually. If tracks are hoaxed, then why don't hoaxers operate in areas of less than twenty inches of precipitation? Further, indicating the unlikeliness of all tracks being hoaxed, Dr. Grover Krantz, who was a physical anthropologist at Washington State University, has calculated that it would take about one thousand different hoaxers, over the years, and over the entire country an average of two weeks a year to create all the tracks that have been found. That seems to me like a large chore for hoaxers.

In 1998, Dr. W. Henner Fahrenbach, a thirty-year veteran of the Oregon National Primate Center, wrote one of the few peer-reviewed scientific-level Bigfoot papers in existence. It was related to the size and scaling of a large sample of Bigfoot tracks cast in Washington and northwest Oregon, primarily during the 1980s and 1990s. In short, Dr.

Fahrenbach developed a scientific method of using footprints and their size to calculate the height and weight of a Bigfoot.

East-central West Virginia, possible Bigfoot track that was very fresh. Always put something in a picture for a size comparison

BERGMANN'S RULE

In nonscientific terms, this rule states that the warmer the area, the smaller the animal; warm-climate animals are generally smaller than their cold-weather counterparts. For example, on average deer in Florida are smaller than deer in Canada. It seems with the information available at present, Bigfoot tracks found in Florida are smaller than in Canada, average wise. Tracks found somewhere in between those two areas are "in between" in average size.

Thousands of tracks have been found and cast over the years. Sure, some have been faked, and many of those are recognized by investigators. Are the hoaxers making such a great effort to make sure they can put the appropriately sized print as they travel? Arguments otherwise don't even make sense and seem disingenuous.

I have spoken to three respected Florida Bigfoot investigators, Diane Stocking, Cathy Betz, and Joanna Cuva. They believe that

Bigfoot in most of Florida are of similar size as elsewhere in the country. However, Betz and Cuva also believe that Bigfoot found in the Everglades swamp are smaller, supporting Bergmann's rule.

AUDIO

This is an up-and-coming part of Bigfoot research. Many researchers, including my good friends "Monongahela," Jim Sherman, Dr. Kenny Brown, and David Ellis are doing presentations and teaching people how not only to record, but to interpret the results. Many are using long-term recorders (LDRs) that can record about six weeks of sound, which can then be analyzed with computer software. In different parts of the country, sounds have led to the discovery of footprints soon after the sounds were recorded.

There is a consistency throughout North America in the sounds recovered, beginning with the earliest recordings known. Those were made in 1972 and for several years after in the Sierra Nevada Mountains of California and were captured by hunters who had a camp many miles from the nearest beaten path. One of the hunters, Ron Morehead, has now made them available in an audio titled "The Sierra Sounds."

To end this short but important discussion on audio, I leave the reader with one final point. Nowadays, audio analysts can infer the size of the animal making the recordings. And some skeptical analysts have come to believe there is definitely something out there vocalizing that has not been recognized by science.

HISTORICAL ACCOUNTS

Going back centuries, Native American tribes and Canadian First Peoples accepted Bigfoot as part of nature and their culture. They have left us hundreds of legends and accounts of the Forest People. Bigfoot is ingrained deep in their cultures. Indeed, Bigfoot language linguist Scott Nelson states that there are six hundred different names of Bigfoot documented in living and extinct Native American languages.

So Native Americans leave no doubt they believe that something is out there.

In Canadian and United States newspapers dating back into the 1800s there are accounts of Bigfoot-type creatures and wild men. Many of these newspaper articles were found by Chad Arment and reproduced in his book *The Historical Bigfoot*. I am honored that Mr. Arment allowed the use of three of his articles in Appendix 1: Wild Men and Giants in addition to a West Virginia article from the author's files.

While names from languages and historical news accounts are anecdotal evidence, they are signals shared by hundreds of tribes of Native Americans, Canadian First Peoples, and European pioneers that Bigfoot is part of the North American past. In my opinion, while this anecdotal evidence is not scientific, it should be given a certain amount of weight, however small, that Bigfoot may have existed in the past.

DNA

There have been unknown hairs. There are even government agencies reporting unknown hair. However, there are several large problems with genetic comparisons. The main problem is that because Bigfoot has not been shown to exist, we have no DNA sample to compare the identified hairs to, no "type" with which to create a baseline.

Aside from this fundamental weakness, there are other problems. For one, the center portion of the hair from which much of the genetic material comes (the medulla) has very little material in it. In addition, Bigfoot hair is not generally found in clumps but instead in single hairs. Rarer still are hairs with attached root bulbs. Mitochondrial DNA comes from the medulla of the hair shaft, while the nuclear DNA comes from the bulb or root of the hair. Lastly, funding is an issue. If you can find an accepting lab, and that's a big if, and it's willing to do the test for you, it costs money, sometimes more than most individuals can afford. There are probably hundreds across the country right now to be tested, but who will pay for testing them? If it comes back as "unidentified primate," as several have to date, few people will be convinced. We can put out hair traps till we die, and no one will care.

Since I first wrote this book, we now have eDNA, *e* standing for environmental. Essentially this is material that has been shed in land or water in the form of skin, excrement, etc. and is tested by new molecular methods. It's been around a little while, but Bigfooters are hopeful as always. In theory you could take a sample of water and tell everything that's in it, or take an area of earth and tell what has walked there. Hypothetically, you could see a Bigfoot standing in a spot and go take a scoop of dirt from where it was and identify an unidentified primate (because remember, Bigfoot hasn't been identified).

Some of the issues that need to be worked through are the testing is better when identifying known species and can look for them more closely, which is helpful with invasives such as, say, snakehead fish. The samples degrade quickly. Testing isn't readily available to the public. And, of course, the ongoing cost considerations. On a positive note, this testing is rapidly developing in the past seven years, so who's to say how it will improve in the next seven. Some unforeseen DNA testing of another type, or an improvement in present testing, will undoubtedly come about as well.

In the end I think a body, or a piece of one, will produce acceptance. I'm aware that Dr. Todd Disotell believes it's possible for acceptance of a species without a body by a combination of video, DNA testing (of some type), game camera pictures, and footprint casting documentation. All of these happening at the same location. Frankly, it's hard to imagine that all that could happen, as it's hard to just get one of the pieces.

Eventually, a hunter will shoot one, or a Bigfoot will get hit on the road. Maybe a homeowner or farmer will have one snooping around their property and shoot one. Then, and probably only then, the academics will run out of their classrooms to show their expertise over a subject that they have so long rejected.

But how many people are actually out there looking? Very, very few. And are there professional trackers/hunters afield? I'm sure a few retired people are looking, but there are no known professionals in the search. The small percentage of citizens who are hunters are in the woods a week or two max and then venture only a quarter mile from the road at the farthest (as reported by *Outdoor Life* from a Pennsylvania study). Throw in a few ginseng and mushroom hunters, and hikers staying on their marked trails. Well, you get the idea. Is there enough room for these animals if they exist? Yes. Is there enough room for these animals to exist? Not even a question to the educated.

SCAT ANALYSIS

One source of DNA and parasites that is generally not considered in field research is that of scat (fecal) collection and analysis. Every animal has a distinct intestinal parasite specific to the species. If this parasite is identified and classified from Bigfoot scat, then a substantial step toward species classification will be accomplished.

For instance, Ivan Sanderson wrote in 1968 that he had firsthand knowledge of a quantity of scat that was shipped in a plastic container surrounded by dry ice across the Atlantic Ocean to Professor W. C. Osman Hill, who was a senior scientist at the London Zoological Museum. He was quoted as saying:

"I wish we had space to give you the report in full. It is quite amazing. The points of significance in it are as follows: In general, this fecal mass did not resemble any known North American animal. On the other hand, it did look humanoid, but it had some peculiar features, as if the lower bowel had a spiral twist. But above all, it was composed exclusively of vegetable matter, and this as far as could be identified of local California freshwater plants. The real clincher, however, was that it contained the eggs and desiccated remains of a certain larvae known only in (a) some Indian tribal groups found in the Northwest, (b) pigs imported from southwest China, (c) human beings in country districts in southwest China, and (d) in pigs in that same area."

Parasites aside, could this aid in the argument of ancestral Bigfoot migrating from southwest China and crossing the Ice Age land bridge? Indeed, a recent femur bone find at Maludong, Yunnan Province, in southwest China strongly indicates an unclassified hominid lived there alongside *Homo sapiens* as recently as fourteen thousand years ago. Fourteen thousand years ago was the Late Pleistocene timeframe in which the Siberian-Alaskan Ice Age land bridge was in use by both large four-legged animals such as mastodons, *Homo sapiens*, and probably, ancestors of our Bigfoot.

Three Scat Mentions in the Literature

In Joe Beelart's book *The Oregon Bigfoot Highway*, he cites two instances of scat analysis by veterinarian laboratories, which found and specified unclassified hominid parasites. However, no science was applied to those findings. Beelart notes that if you properly collect a probable Bigfoot scat sample, don't freeze it. Freezing kills intestinal parasites and was the specific cause of both samples in his book not being analyzed a second time. In addition, some scientists recommend trying to collect the end of the stool that was the last to come out, as it may contain more epithelial/anal cells.

In addition, anal lubricating oils may also contain DNA specific to Bigfoot. Mr. Peter Byrne in his recollections of fifty years of Bigfoot research points out that DNA is now collected from elephant scat anal lubricating oils and tissues, superseding the old, sometime injurious dart-with-drugs method. Byrne speculates that carefully selected Bigfoot scat samples may also yield DNA.

Byrne is very correct in stating the utmost care must be made in selecting and properly collecting scat samples. Beelart pointed out in one case, gigantic size was the deciding factor in the selection process and subsequent request for analysis. In the other instance, the scat was located next to a Bigfoot's fern bed where a fisherman had a terrifying encounter.

On another matter not relating to scat, just finding Bigfoot scat might provide a wealth of information. The location where it is found allows us to see why they may be in a particular area, whether it be for feeding or traveling, and allows us to look for similar locations. Food-stuffs contained in the scat lets the researcher know where the animal has been and what he has eaten at particular times of the year and locations.

The reader should know that it's hard to find what may be Bigfoot scat. There are reports of Bigfoot being latrine-like with their scat, meaning they go to the same area repetitiously when in an area. There are also reports of Bigfoot standing in water when they go to the bath-room. I've only found scat on two occasions that I didn't recognize and believed may be from a Bigfoot. Of course, the bacteria in the waste immediately begin to break down the material and thus the DNA, creating another challenge.

One must understand the complications of collecting a mass of fresh, foul-smelling, large scat (assuming you're lucky enough to find it) and get it to a DNA lab (it's hard to find one and expensive), unfrozen, before the sample is useless. This is another reason that research by the government or universities may yield better or more promising results.

In the 70s they began searching tree breaks for hair samples.
Using a magnifying glass can help identify vermin damaging the tree

Image Copyright Sybilla Irwin 2013

This Bigfoot was seen within eyeshot of the world famous New River gorge bridge.
Illustration by Sybilla Irwin

CHAPTER 5
WHAT IS IT?

"You're talking about the Yeti, Bigfoot, or Sasquatch; you'll be amazed when I tell you that I'm sure they exist." Jane Goodall, primatologist, and the world's foremost expert on chimpanzees

IF THERE IS A BIGFOOT, WHAT EXACTLY IS IT?

Many researchers have long considered spending their time getting acknowledgment for Bigfoot in general before worrying about what the Bigfoot is specifically. Clearly with citizen scientists, this is the order in which things would happen. Scientifically, most scientists want a reasonable possibility of a lineage that makes sense, not to mention hard evidence to go with it, meaning most likely a body or a piece of a body. That being said, I believe the best contenders for Bigfoot's lineage are as follows.

GIGANTOPITHECUS

Gigantopithecus was a large ape similar to and in the family of an orangutan. Originally from Asia, it was discovered in 1935 when a paleontologist was looking through a Chinese apothecary in Hong

Kong and found a very large molar tooth. Since that time, about a thousand teeth and a couple of partial jaws of *Gigantopithecus* have been found in Asia. The theory would be that *Gigantopithecus*, an herbivore, migrated across the Bering Land Bridge like many other species. It evolved to become an omnivore, meaning to eat both plant and animal matter. *Gigantopithecus blacki* is the most common and largest of the species, but there is a *Gigantopithecus giganteus*, which is roughly half the size, but is a relatively unknown species because of the lack of fossils to study.

There is a lot to like about the "Giganto" lineage. It is a large ape nine to ten feet tall, approaching 1,200 pounds, or roughly half if you choose the *giganteus* species. Many species, including humans, crossed the Bering Land Bridge during the last Ice Age, and *Gigantopithecus* could have been one of them. It would be in the orangutan family, which are shy, solitary animals living in isolated areas. Animals so widely dispersed seldom produce remains that are found, and in the case of many other mammals, the remains are often covered with brush and stones. The greatest number of Bigfoot reports describe an animal with reddish-brown hair similar to that of an orangutan. orangutans are intelligent creatures who are curious about humans and their behavior.

But there are also problems with the "Giganto" theory. There is much debate about whether *Gigantopithecus* was ever bipedal. In addition, *Gigantopithecus* was an herbivore, and no evidence of its presence has been found in the Americas. That wouldn't be surprising even if it was proven to exist. I'm not as concerned about the lack of fossil evidence, as there should be millions and millions of bones in Asia, and only a couple of shopping bags of bones have been found. Most of the bony remainders of animals, the bones that are not dissolved by nature or disintegrated by animals and insects, will naturally decompose, and disappear in five to ten years anyway, making it unlikely for a scientist to ever come into contact with them. For example, many excavated Native American Indian mounds in North America were found to have few or no bones in them due to the soil not being conducive to preserving bony remains. And lastly, keep in mind that we have none of that evidence for gorillas, and just got it for chimpanzees, and they obviously exist and in great numbers.

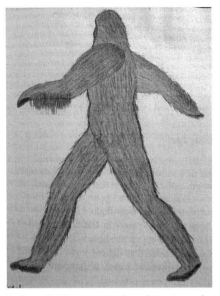

Witness sketch made 17 years after the sighting for author. Witness said he had done hundreds of sketches. He emphasized the long forearm hair, which is very common to hear, and reddish-brown hair

PARANTHROPUS

Specifically, *Paranthropus robustus*, found in South Africa, *P. robustus* is characterized by well-developed jaws and chewing muscles that are supported by attaching high on the skull to form a sagittal crest. *P. robustus* lived at the same time as *Gigantopithecus* and *Homo erectus*, and one possible belief is that Bigfoot may be *P. robustus* or a closely related descendent.

Paranthropus was a woodland creature that was heavily muscled and bipedal. There exists some evidence that *Paranthropus* was an omnivore.

There are problems with this theory, as all fossils of Paranthropus have been found in Africa, so it would have to come much farther to get to North America, and we don't have any proof along the path it would have had to take. In addition, *Paranthropus* was generally less than five feet tall, and its brain was 40% smaller than a modern human's brain. I don't necessarily believe that Bigfoot's brain is the size of modern humans', but based on its ability to avoid detection, I think it's reasonable to expect a fairly moderate brain size. In addition, usually the larger the animal, the larger the brain size. For instance, body size is often cited as the reason Neanderthals, who were very thick and heavily muscled, had larger brains than modern humans.

THE HOMO LINE

Anytime that someone brings up the *Homo* family, we jump to the conclusion that they are saying that Bigfoot is human. The suspicion that Bigfoot is of the *Homo* line doesn't suggest Bigfoot is the same species as modern humans (*Homo sapiens*). I have spent a lot of time researching the possibilities surrounding the *Homo*-Bigfoot lineage. The reason that there continues to be a growing interest in the tie-in is primarily bipedalism. Bipedalism, meaning walking on two legs, is an unusual trait in nature and, as such, makes one consider that Bigfoot must come from the *Homo* line about the time that bipedalism developed. It that were the case, Bigfoot would be tied around the *Homo erectus* family.

A famous example of *Homo erectus* is Peking man. The timing is right, as is the location; Peking man could have easily crossed the Bering Land Bridge. *Homo erectus* lived approximately 1.8 million to 70,000 years ago, which is, like, no time at all. Many branches exist in order to get to *Homo sapiens*. In theory, for Bigfoot to have come from the *Homo* line, it diverged long ago based on Bigfoot's lack of use of fire and tools. Could this possibility be the reason that some of the DNA that has been tested comes back as human? For the most part, Bigfoot researchers have assumed faulty handling of the sample in these cases, but it could be that the DNA is closely related to *Homo sapiens* through *Homo erectus*. If Bigfoot exists, then it is in all likelihood that its DNA is the closest known to modern human DNA.

As with so many of these possibilities, the problem is a lack of fossil evidence to show either the lineage or evidence that the primate (other than modern humans) walked across the land bridge to North America. Once again, conditions and locations have to be just right for fossils to develop. At the end of the day, we don't know anyone who has actually gone out to search for Bigfoot fossils or Bigfoot bones.

Is it possible that Bigfoot is a living fossil like the coelacanth fish found in 1938 off the coast of South Africa? A so-called "living fossil" is the only remaining member of a group that is otherwise extinct. The coelacanth was thought to be dead for sixty-five million years. In a similar way, the peccary, a small piglike animal whose habitat stretches south from the southwestern United States, was found long after it was thought to be extinct. If Bigfoot is an *H. erectus* family member, it is a living fossil.

A GREAT APE

An ape that is obviously unknown at this point probably would be related to the ancestral orang, or maybe some offshoot of *Gigantopithecus*, which was related to the orangutans. There are large monkeys in the Himalayas, so theoretically, it would be possible for an ape to adapt to a more temperate existence. Such an ape would have had to cross the land bridge and become an omnivore and done so in such small numbers that its fossil past is either nonexistent or not identified. It would have lived in small pockets and in areas of great biodiversity. Of course, we have no evidence of such an animal existing in the past, but it seems as reasonable and plausible as the other alternatives.

This line of speculation makes me wonder how smart Bigfoot actually is. We are talking about an animal that has been around at least as long as man. It avoids detection by man; it can apparently stay hidden. Hearing game cameras and being nocturnal aren't necessarily functions of intelligence but rather a survival adaptation. A chimpanzee has a brain one-third the size of modern man's yet uses tools. Perhaps a better approach to determining Bigfoot's lineage would be to figure out the intelligence suspected of Bigfoot and see where it matches up with existing primate species. Once there, we may have a better idea of what they are capable of, and maybe that will lend a hand in procuring better and consistent evidence.

Fayette County, West Virginia. With the exception of the tallest mountains water in Appalachia is always plentiful

CHAPTER 6
MATTERS OF HOT DEBATE

CONTROVERSIAL SUBJECTS IN THE BIGFOOT FIELD

"Skepticism is the best quality a researcher can have." Thomas Steenburg, *Bigfoot researcher*

BIGFOOT KNOCKING SOUNDS

Many believe and it's generally accepted that Bigfoot makes knocking sounds. What the knocks mean is not known for sure, but they are believed to be a method of communication. Perhaps the knocks are saying, "Danger! Someone is here!" Or maybe something like, "I am here. Where are you?" Some believe it is relaying how many people are in the woods, something like, "Three people are here." Maybe it's repeated when someone leaves?

How exactly the knocking sound is made is also a point of contention. Some people believe that a Bigfoot may have a stick and walks around the woods, hitting the sides of trees. Personally, I have a hard time believing that a Bigfoot walks around the woods carrying a stick with him or her to be ready to knock at all times, but there have been a couple of witnesses who supposedly saw this taking place.

Another possibility is that the knock is made by a tongue or mouth pop, the art of making a loud noise with one's mouth. Some monkeys and apes make this type of sound. Lastly, some believe that the knocking sound is actually a hand clap, an action that has been observed in monkeys and apes. Ever been around one of those people who clap their hands so loud its annoying? Imagine hands a couple of sizes larger than human hands, like a Bigfoot has, and the amount of noise they could make with those mitts?!

A "homerun" knock is one that is very close to you and so loud that it vibrates right through you. It's so close that if it's in the daylight, you expect to see the animal. I have been around for one of those and believe it to be far too loud for a hand clap or a mouth pop. In all likelihood, all three ways to make a knock may well be used depending upon the circumstances.

Speaking of homerun knocks, I was leading three groups in the woods one night near Canaan Valley State Park in West Virginia, and when coming out of the woods late at night, I heard one. All three groups of people, around thirty, were blended together while walking out. All at once there was an enormous homerun knock not fifty yards from us just over the hill. It startled everyone, and only three people stayed there! Later many said that the sound was much louder than they anticipated, and it caught them off guard.

TREE BENDS, BREAKS, STRUCTURES, ARCHES, AND APPARENT PLACEMENT

This topic is probably one of the most debated. Many Bigfoot enthusiasts go into the woods strictly looking at trees. I think such people get the evidence thing backwards. I believe hunting for evidence of Bigfoot should be approached in the same way a jury hears evidence: a defendant is innocent until proven guilty. Ideally, investigators don't look for evidence against a person; they go where the evidence takes them. Bigfoot hunting should follow the evidence; unfortunately, some people view certain "evidence," like tree bends for instance, as solid evidence of the presence of Bigfoot. The reality is that tree bends and tree breaks happen in the woods all the time, for a variety of reasons. I call it "woods litter." Bigfoot researcher Joe Beelart, author of *The Oregon Bigfoot Highway*, believes it so rarely involves Bigfoot that it is "one in a million."

I'm afraid that much of the talk of tree structures has been repeated so often that people believe it to be fact. Many of the seasoned older researchers, like Thomas Steenburg of British Columbia, believe tree structures have very little to do with Bigfoot. Now, do I believe that Bigfoot doesn't ever mess with trees? No, I am impressed by some twisted trees, broken trees, and some trees shoved in the ground sometimes and on occasion. It's been reported that all of the great apes habitually bend, break, and snap off trees. I have had investigators with stories of trees being driven top first into the ground and other instances that surely must be Bigfoot related or may even appear Bigfoot related. I am also convinced there are other Bigfoot-related events surrounding tree structures. Was there a Bigfoot seen or heard around the mystery finding? Was a track found nearby? That would make it compelling and indicative to me.

Another concern I have with so many findings related to supposed Bigfoot structures or elements is the lack of history among the American Indians and First Nations peoples. They have generations of stories about Bigfoot and their behavior but no mention of this purported Bigfoot behavior. I also commonly make the argument that if these tree or stick manipulations were common, then our forefathers, the hunters and outdoorsman who had to be outdoors to live, would have noticed and talked of these things, but alas, nothing has been communicated from them to us. I, once again, believe that it happens but far less than what we are being led to believe on social media and by some authors.

Walk into the large forests of West Virginia and there is tree litter (sorry I didn't come up with a better term) literally surrounding you at all times except in the very oldest of forests, few of which exist anymore. Almost everything everywhere has been timbered. Bob Titmus (1918–1997), one of the oldest and most seasoned Bigfoot researchers in the modern era, stated that with the help of one other person, he could twist a two-inch tree to exactly what many people are seeing in the woods. I'm sure that some of the people hoax some of the bends, arches, twist, etc. All of these explanations are reasons why it is so important to have some other Bigfoot-related activity to correlate with tree bends and structures. Nature does really weird and unusual things under even the most ordinary of circumstances. Ever notice how many of these structures are located in pine forests? Pine forests that have notoriously shallow roots and trees that will dance in storms. Either Bigfoot spends an inordinate time in pine forests, or some researchers are being fooled by common happenings in these types of woods. Bigfoot are rare and isolated, and evidence of their passing is the same.

Tree with the top pinned into ground far enough to make an arch.
A Bigfoot sign or just the magic of nature?

NESTS

I believe that sometimes Bigfoot will make a bed of nesting materials such as fern, pine, and grasses. Nests are not found often but are usually in an area with an overlook and may also be found in a rock structure like a cave or an overhang. They have been found all over North America. Some supposed Bigfoot nests have interwoven branches, which require manual dexterity.

It is important for us to keep in mind that bears build nests, and that must be considered first upon finding a large nest. There are many, many more bears than Bigfoot, so nests are much more likely to be bear nests than Bigfoot nests. Bear nests are smaller, three by five feet, as bears on average tend to be smaller, around two hundred pounds.

Probably the most well-known of the nests are the relatively recent finds of the Olympic Project. A great number of complicated, large nests were found by a surveyor. A lot of scientists who have looked at the nests were intrigued. eDNA was performed without any compelling results, but like any new technology, implementation in the field has a learning curve. Nests have been found for decades, and in all areas of North America, but I suspect more aren't found due to humans sticking to trails and not venturing in remote hard-to-get-to areas. I've found one nest in southeast Ohio, and my impression was it was active. I've also found a bed of two animals that I believed to be a Bigfoot based on a track and finding a stack of walnuts nearby that were obviously placed where they were located. One was a little larger than a bear size and the other the size of a car hood. They were located on a sidehill about two miles from the nearest house. It was over a hill from a right-of-way that had loads of berries at the time and no four-wheeler traffic. It was donut shaped and apparent that something heavy was using it.

I found this by following my belief that in warm, berry-producing months, it is common to find Bigfoot on north-facing hillsides, not in the main hollow, which will also have a seep or spring nearby. I was looking for rights-of-way that four-wheelers couldn't access that had berries. I look at OnX or Google Earth and find these places and then boots on the ground to investigate. I just start at the bottom and work my way back and forth. Like everything else Bigfoot, it's more common to find nothing than it is to find something suspect.

EVERYTHING IS BIGFOOT

Habituation refers to human-Bigfoot encounters, sightings, vocalizations, or track finds that recur, sometimes happening over a period of weeks, months, or even years. In a typical case of habituation, a person will leave some token treat food, such as blueberries, table scraps, toys, rocks, etc. in a predetermined location. It could be in back of their house, on a stump or a rock, etc. Some call this "gifting." Regardless, there is an attempt to interact with something. At a later time the person goes back and may find what they left out gone, altered, or something left in its place. I would define a habituator as someone who intentionally interacts with something he or she believes to be a Bigfoot through feeding, games, and curiosity ploys. There are many prominent researchers who don't believe this may be possible. Others believe that maybe the Bigfoot is training the humans.

Strange as it may seem, these habituation cases happen all over the country. Not all of the cases are real. Some people make the claims up to get attention. Some are feeding other animals and believe the disappearing or altered food/objects to be caused by Bigfoot.

One of the problems is that after the initial experience, the witness begins to equate nearly everything with Bigfoot. Investigators encounter this all the time. I'm not sure whether it's that the "witnesses" want the investigator to believe them, or they just want to have a really good story. I don't believe in most cases they are being deceitful on purpose. Maybe it's because Bigfoot encounters are so rare that the witnesses don't really know what is reasonable. Maybe they have researched the "woo" factor, or the paranormal part of the field, which so terrifies our participating scientists.

All that said, I still believe that in a real case of habituation it may be possible to acquire some of the very best evidence. However, will it really matter to the public and the scientists unless it's a body? It should be noted that for all the people who claim habituation situations, we have yet to receive more than anecdotal claims at this point.

What we know for certain is that people hunting Bigfoot must always wear their "skepticals." If you are near a stream or pond and hear something splash, in all likelihood it is a fish or a beaver, not a Bigfoot throwing something at you. If something in the woods drops beside you, it's probably a stick falling out of a tree and not a Bigfoot throwing a rock or nut. As all first-year medical students are taught, when making a diagnosis, if you hear hoofbeats, think horse not zebra. We need to bring cynicism into our research. That does not mean to disregard someone or not document a story if it seems too far out there. The standard of proof must be high for what most assume is a mythical or cultural animal. For something that is a great claim, and surely an unacknowledged bipedal primate is, great evidence is required.

Recently, I was looking at pictures with a group of people. They were checking out a tree about four inches in diameter that had been snapped off about eight feet off the ground. There was an assumption it was Bigfoot related, although there was no other Bigfoot evidence beyond the tree break.

Those people had to ask themselves questions that brought their cynicism to bear: (a) What type of tree was it? (b) What types of pests or insects bother that tree? (c) Where in the tree do these pests usually damage or attack? (d) Can wind, ice, or snow be ruled out as a cause?

It is important to do research beyond looking to see if there are other trees in the area that look the same way. Look at the evidence from a scientific standpoint rather than from that of a simple Bigfoot enthusiast. Enthusiasm will never convince anyone, other than another Bigfoot enthusiast, of Bigfoot's existence!

A lot of my hikes are planned in areas that I can find remote beaver dams. Dams are nature's smorgasbords

ANYONE HAVE A PICTURE OF A BIRD IN THEIR GAME CAMERA?

Aside from all the problems that we have talked about previously, we must remember that a game camera picture of Bigfoot is a matter of perspective. It's very hard to tell the depth of field when looking at a game camera picture. Insects up close to the lens may look large. Squirrel whiskers up close to the camera can look like fur and hair from a larger animal. Bears often approach game cameras, and in the night with a flash, a bear's hair up close can appear to be something else—like a Bigfoot. Some of the most controversial pictures of Bigfoot look to me like birds in varying forms, either landing or taking off. Camera angles can also distort the form of birds and other subjects. Remember those illusion drawings where you see an old woman in a fur coat or a beautiful young woman in a hat? It's all about perspective, and perspective is particularly difficult to gain from game cameras.

I remember one photo that the *Finding Bigfoot* television show was investigating that showed a supposed Bigfoot standing by a hunting shack. In the foreground of the picture were crows. Conclusion: A crow in a form of flight. We don't always have the tools that academics would use to study these images, and individuals often see what they want to see.

Inside the Bigfoot Field Researchers Organization, we debate many of these pictures for months before the public ever sees them. Many times, we know the backstory, which usually never comes out. Sometimes a photo of a bird will show up in the media as "showing a possible Bigfoot" when the picture has been debunked. This has happened to me. A witness sent a photo that looked like a possible Bigfoot but was really a bird in a stage of flight. I explained it to the witness, showed them how it worked, and left thinking they understood. Six months later the photo was on the front page of a magazine and on the internet as a new Bigfoot photo!

BIGFOOT SIGHTINGS ARE GOING DOWN

There have been reports saying the number of Bigfoot sightings is going down. Is it possible that Bigfoot is an endangered species and is going extinct? Maybe, but I doubt it. I think a couple of different things are actually going on.

Matt Moneymaker, TV star and founder of the BFRO, is in many of the state and national parks across the country. Prior to Covid, he says that he had never seen fewer people hiking and camping than at that time, and he attributed the decrease in sightings to the lack of possible witnesses. Ironically, during Covid, people were in our state and national parks like they hadn't been in a long time, and sightings went up during that period. I do know that when I hike deep into the woods, like I do a couple of times a week, I seldom see anyone deep in the woods.

A few weeks ago in the Sunday paper (do they even exist anymore?), there was an article about how afraid of the outdoors our population is. Never in our history have so few people been outdoors. They have lost touch with that part of their existence. They are afraid of the woods, the dark, and the animals that are out there. To have a

Bigfoot sighting, a witness must be there. If a Bigfoot walks through a forest, but no one's there to see it, has there been a Bigfoot sighting? Obviously not.

I believe that some of the people who watch the Bigfoot television shows do so because they have had an experience that they believe to be Bigfoot related. When these shows became really popular, a lot of people felt their need to report their sighting. Maybe there was less stigma attached to the subject than before. When the internet first came along, many people had a chance to report a Bigfoot sighting they had experienced previously. As a result of these factors, many historical reports surfaced. Now, while we still get older reports, the majority of the reports are more recent. There were simply more reports to be had and reported a couple of decades ago.

THE SCIENTIST VERSUS THE ENTHUSIAST

Keep in mind that I am speaking in generalities. Scientists have a hard time accepting Bigfoot or, in some cases, saying it publicly, because admitting it can affect their professional reputation and their future in their field. Academia in general can be stodgy and slow to change. The amount of evidence needed by science to accept Bigfoot far exceeds acceptance in other quarters. If thousands of witnesses came forward to testify to a premise, it would be accepted. The famous researcher and author John Green said that "a formal legal inquiry, if it could be arranged, would almost certainly declare that the present available evidence conclusively demonstrates the existence of Sasquatch."

Academics are seldom in the field; academics are seldom engaged. The enthusiast, on the other hand, believes and forms his opinions based on a belief. The enthusiast works the evidence backwards. He or she is generally uneducated on nature and ecology and, as a result, doesn't always understand what they are looking at. Therefore, what enthusiasts may or may not find is shaped by their beliefs rather than any formal training.

The enthusiast seldom has equipment but rather just puts in time walking, screaming, hitting trees, and sitting around a campfire listening. I admire the enthusiast's energy and persistence. I just believe that if an enthusiast is really interested, he or she should take some classes. Learn more about nature: plants, animals, terrain, weather, the whole mix. Many states offer master naturalist and/or master gardener training at nominal costs. There are also tracking classes available across the country.

A setup I use in remote locations. Pinning some treat or colorful item to a tree with duct tape. I have been able to get hair off the duct tape but most of the time nothing happens.

If we don't do these things, then when Bigfoot is found to be real and acknowledged by science, the academics and professionals will come out from behind their desks and take over the research. They will be allowed in areas others aren't, and get paid to do it. The enthusiast who spends at most a week or two spread out over weekends in a year, doing the same things that people have been doing over the last fifty years, will continue to provide anecdotal experiences but little to no evidence. But for right now, most of the interest is in the hands and hearts of the weekend warrior enthusiasts. Let's educate ourselves and evolve in what we do!

CHAPTER 7
21ST-CENTURY BIGFOOTERY

"I think Bigfoot is blurry, that's the problem. There is a large out-of-focus 'monster' roaming the countryside." Mitch Hedbert, comedian

HOW THE INTERNET AND TELEVISION HAVE CHANGED REPORTS

Imagine what it was like in the "old days" to get or file a Bigfoot report. Everything was strictly word of mouth. Then came the internet, and all of a sudden people were able to look up national and local groups in order to file a report. Most of the early reports were BFRO "Class A," that is, reports that are visual. There is no doubt on the part of the witness; he or she believes they saw a Bigfoot very clearly. With the ability to read other reports, people began to hear about other incidents that others were having, and recognized something that had happened as a possible Bigfoot event. Now, putting these reports together, Bigfoot actually seems to have a behavior instead of just a creature seen fleetingly.

Eventually, we began to get an occasional Bigfoot television show and sometimes even a series. The popularity of the shows and Bigfoot in pop culture caused an influx of reports. With public education came the "Class B" and "Class C" reports. These are possible sightings and noise-only types of activity or maybe where someone didn't see something really clearly, maybe something more anecdotal. Fortunately, many witnesses are now able to recognize purported Bigfoot sounds. Unfortunately, the public is seldom outside. Also, often the public does not recognize common nighttime animal and bird sounds, and they often confuse them for Bigfoot sounds. I suspect a great many sounds witnesses believe are Bigfoot sounds are actually foxes, coyotes, or owls.

So we receive a lot more reports now than before the internet, but they must be sifted through more rigorously. Many times, just talking with a witness makes it easy to sort it out. Without some corroborating evidence, sounds by themselves should not be trusted as much as other types of reports. Still, sounds should be kept in mind, particularly when considering their location.

Because Bigfoot is popular and there may be a chance to gain notoriety or even get on television, hoaxes can be an issue. However, I don't think that the great majority of the people are interested in faking a report or hoaxing in general, but rather they just misinterpret what they saw or heard. That's been my experience when meeting witnesses. The vast majority of the people want no fame or fortune, just answers to what happened to them. They want to talk about what happened to them and tell someone who will believe them. Many do not want anyone to know their names. I had a couple of witnesses who could have been on the *Finding Bigfoot* television show but turned it down because they didn't want their identity to become public. One was a teacher and the other a police officer.

The witnesses who bother me the most are the ones who get away. There are witnesses who leave great messages and emails that show that they are bright and well spoken. Sometimes they have second thoughts about talking and break contact, and I'm disappointed by that. Other times they retract their report because they don't want the public scrutiny, or as one woman told me, "I don't want people on my land, messing with these things."

THE GREAT LOGAN COUNTY COAL MINER HOAX

I had an interesting hoax several years ago. When a report comes in, it goes to the able secretary of the BFRO, Caroline Curtis. Caroline is an investigator, expedition organizer, and the glue that holds things together. She helps new members with their reports and the existing investigators with any of their needs. Caroline sent me an email with a series of voice messages sent in by a reported witness from Logan, West Virginia. I called him, and we talked for an hour. He lives at the base of a mountain near Chief Logan State Park in southwest West Virginia. I was intimately familiar with the area, as I had spent several months hiking in and around that park. He relayed that something had been stealing food from an outside freezer, including a turkey and deer meat. This is something that has been commonly reported across the country. He stated that he had heard a noise and went outside to see a female and a male Bigfoot. He had pictures of footprints, but they were on the side of a steep bank and hard to see clearly. I wrote a long note about the interview and sent it out to a group of investigators for them to review and suggest questions. I called the witness back for another conversation and set up a visit. Before I left for the visit, I reviewed maps to be familiar with the land.

The supposed witness was a coal miner. When I met him, he had a large buck knife on his side, which is always disconcerting when just meeting someone and going deep into the woods. He had one of those nervous and quirky personalities that just jumps from one subject to another. He also lectured me on the size of the scrotum of an orang-utan in comparison to other primates because he believed he saw the entire package of the Bigfoot he'd supposedly observed.

When I got there, I wanted to know, "Why would a Bigfoot be at this place rather than thousands of other places in the state?" The truth was I didn't think that one would be there. It was close to a main road, neighbors were everywhere with dogs, and many had motion lights, and a witness who was good on the phone but poor in person. Unfortunately, I decided that his report was hoaxed. In these cases, I avoid confrontation at all costs and simply thank the "witness" and tell him his report is valuable and will be placed in the BFRO files for other investigators to look at.

Other witnesses can just be a little out there (or a lot). I had a woman who knew she had a family of Bigfoot living on her land but didn't want to tell me where she lived because the Hells Angels Motorcycle Club had been bothering her.

I also have had two witnesses who claimed to have shot a Bigfoot. Luckily, the last gentleman was able to hit the Bigfoot with twenty-one out of twenty-four shots, or his life would have been endangered. Unfortunately for science, the Bigfoot was able to get away.

There are a lot of hoaxers in the public right now. Many have made some television time and others money from their claims. Some have achieved notoriety. I think the biggest problem is that a certain percentage of the population is simply naïve. Another problem is that all of us want to believe and help get evidence so, so badly.

It's hard to be objective when you're the one getting a particular piece of evidence. We have well-known people in the Bigfoot field who associate with people who are well-known hoaxers, and that's hard to understand. We don't accept the well-known, public image of the "Bigfoot person" to be someone seen hanging out with the wrong people. It kills whatever credibility and goodwill Bigfoot researchers have attained in the public's eyes, not to mention their standing within the Bigfoot community.

I suspect that many of the hoaxers are in areas with some Bigfoot activity and probably have experienced some themselves. From what I have seen on television, hoaxing is the type of activity that anyone experienced in the field would be able to put out for you in an active Bigfoot area. Some hoaxers have seen or produced just enough evidence to seem believable, but they can't help themselves, and their story and experiences keep evolving. Don't forget that many of these people started by filing a BFRO report in the first place, got interviewed by an investigator, so they are well known by the organization. We many times sit on the sidelines, watching or listening to an interview or reading an article, knowing that the person isn't telling the truth.

It's challenging to get good evidence. Often the animal has been in the area for generations and know far better than Bigfoot "hunters" and residents the places where people don't go. I believe there are so few Bigfoot in the first place, and as primates with higher intelligence than most animals in the woods, Bigfoot are especially hard to find. The technology needed for Bigfoot research to even the score is expensive and hard to implement in the field. We investigators have a saying: when Bigfooting, whatever can go wrong with the equipment will go wrong.

For instance, you're on an expedition. You get out of a vehicle, and there is a "wood knock" before you even get the recorder going. A lot of nights it's wet and cold, and the batteries die at the most inopportune time. One night investigator Darren Pevarnik and I were in a remote location with no one around for miles. Darren had set up his thermal imager on our camp to keep watch and record while we slept. I had put a game camera inside a cooler, smeared it with blood and peanut butter, and placed it at the edge of the woods near my tent. There are many reports of Bigfoot messing with cameras, so I was hoping to entice one to open my cooler so I could get a face shot.

Sure enough, about 3 a.m. I heard the cooler moving around, it could have been anything, but the sound had my attention. We had left an audio recorder on a picnic table all night, and from the recording, we later heard a grunt and a can of Off! mosquito repellant being moved on the table. It was an interesting event but not enough evidence to make a conclusive statement. The thermal footage? Some glitch with the formatting, and it wasn't retrievable. Once again though, would anyone have believed our footage if we had gotten it? No! Our friends and family would have, but everyone else in the country would have just thought, "It's a human they bumped into or who was hidden out there."

Interest in Bigfoot is huge. The public's appetite for information is insatiable. As with any field not run by scientists, the government, or universities, the standard for evidence varies greatly. If you notice on the website (BFRO.net), the BFRO is specializing in doing scientific research on the subject. We, as investigators, debate these things daily and try to reach a consensus on the evidence at hand.

Unfortunately, weekly on popular websites I see evidence that I know to be fake or severely lacking. Most of the Bigfoot websites vet no evidence at all. I get exhausted on seeing a scrape in the dirt described as a "possible Bigfoot footprint." We need to hold our standards to a higher level. I can assure you that there are scientists who are seriously interested in the phenomena but are looking on the "sly" because they are troubled by some of the weak evidence put forward, not to mention the "woo factor."

OF BEARS AND BIGFOOT

There's an interesting relationship between bears and Bigfoot. Generally, any place you find a Bigfoot is inside the range of bears. I'm mainly speaking of black bears which are found throughout the continent and the only type of bear on the east coast. Many skeptics and naysayers believe many of the Bigfoot sightings to be a bear sighting, and I don't doubt it.

Bears and Bigfoot are the two largest mammals in the woods and it's interesting to consider how they may coexist. Many in the Bigfoot community often wonder if they fight each other, and if they do what that may look like. It's my contention that the two have made adaptations in order to make confrontations less likely and to share habitats without direct conflict.

First, consider that bears were almost gone on the east coast, largely because of hunting, but by the mid-1900s the trend reversed and their numbers grew, mainly due to timbering. I wonder if timbering also helped Bigfoot numbers grow? There's may be a direct correlation between deer population and Bigfoot numbers, similar to bobcats and rabbits. Interestingly, there's more forest now than there was eighty years ago but that's not the public perception.

Let's look at how Bigfoot and bears are alike. They are both k-selected species, meaning they are long-lived, they mature late (meaning how old they are when they reproduce), and have low reproductive rates. Bears reproduce every other year, but we have no idea about Bigfoot reproduction rates other than to say that apes reproduce every few years and orangutans are the least active in producing babies, just once every eight years. Bigfoot is most likely not an annual reproducer.

Both bears and Bigfoot have a wide range distribution but aren't found in high densities. In both group's movement is determined by security and food. They both follow food regarding elevation, where it applies. Meaning, they are lower in elevation in cooler months and may move higher as the weather warms. As the weather cools, the bears are going into hibernation (for six months in the coldest areas) but Bigfoot would be required to follow the food wherever that may be.

Road access by timber, electric, and gas companies into forested areas are the biggest threat to security of the two groups. It allows more access to hunters and less cover. In Ohio, and some other states, electric companies are cutting gravel roads to each set of poles on every right-of-way to make it easier to deal with outages and damage to lines in the future. This is great for humans but in many places like Ohio it is getting continually harder to find the remote and truly wild places.

Gloger's rule, an ecological rule (regarding the color of animals), stated that among warm blooded animals, black is the prevalent color in warm and moist areas. It's interesting to consider if this is relevant for Bigfoot and bears. We can be assured at the very least, color phases are a function of genetics. Bears tend to darken as they age (melanotic), while reports suggest that Bigfoot tend to stay the same color throughout life.

Now for some of the things that differ between bears and Bigfoot, and the allowances that they may make for not coming into contact with each other. Remember these are generalizations as a product of studies, field observations, and witness reports.

Bears tend to avoid ridge lines, upper slopes, and rock formations (talus areas as well). I believe that Bigfoot is found on remote ridges, where humans aren't and tend to bed on slopes (even the steepest slopes have flat spots). Bears tend to den on north slopes, but Bigfoot tend to spend time in cooler weather on south-facing slopes, and especially south facing rocks and cliffs. It seems biologically natural for a warm-blooded mammal to want to get a little of that warm sun if they can.

Bears are the least active between 1-4 AM, whereas those are a very active time for a Bigfoot.

Bears don't use clear cut land until about ten years, which is when that land starts producing a wide variety of food. In places like Ohio, which lacks an abundance of deep woods, I'm inclined to believe that Bigfoot are using clear cuts for security when they become thick, typically a few years after the clearing.

Bears, while omnivores (eating both meat and plant matter), eat only two percent animal matter. It was always believed to be much higher until some recent studies have confirmed how little meat they actually eat. Bigfoot, I theorize, must be more of a true omnivore, as that is largely the only way to accumulate calories in the winter without raiding human houses, trash cans, and the like. One must be a meat eater in those circumstances and that includes roadkill (as often reported), in addition to knowing where a healthy deer population is located.

THE GOOD DOCTOR DOES FINDING BIGFOOT

Television shows have piqued interest and shown the public how to do research, or at the very least make some noises! Prior to the television shows, much of the public had little idea that Bigfoot made sounds. Now you have campers and weekend warriors traveling all over the place doing "wood knocks" and making "howls" and other noises attributed to Bigfoot, hoping for a reply.

Here I should probably talk about television more specifically. I have helped out on three different episodes of *Finding Bigfoot* as well as a number of other producers about possible upcoming shows about Bigfoot.

The first time I helped *Finding Bigfoot* was the first season that they were on. They called me and told me where they were going and wanted me to help get some of my witnesses to come up during filming. Personally, I would have called the Bigfoot Field Researchers Organization investigators in that state and asked, "Where are the hot areas?" The producers of the show had access to the database, but the investigators are talking to people all the time and know the lay of the land, so to speak. They have established relationships in the area with landowners and witnesses. Investigators know many areas not in the database. Nonetheless, we were all happy to help Matt Moneymaker any way that we could. It was important to all of us.

The second episode that I helped with, I got to suggest the best place to go. I handed off all of the witnesses to the show's production crew and found a location for their investigation. It was great to see the cast, but the producers just make you feel in the way when they have what they need. The only request I made was to show West Virginia's beauty when they filmed, and they really did a great job doing that.

The third episode I helped with, I once again got to suggest where to go, but the schedule was based on where they wanted to go, and not on the weather. They bumped the filming so they could film in Michigan because they were worried about snow. Of course, they failed to take into consideration altitude and got snowed on during the West Virginia episode! I realize that there is a schedule, but everyone, including the producers, now recognizes the show can be organized better.

There was a spot that I really wanted them to go to in the New River Gorge that had recent activity that no one knew about. A producer asked me what I thought about another spot:

"Well, it's okay," I said, "but not as good as the location I gave you."

"The other spot is much more convenient for catering and such," she said.

"Well, what's the name of the show?" I felt that if you were really after Bigfoot, then let's go to the best place, but she responded, "Well."

The cast of *Finding Bigfoot* is first class. Matt, Cliff, and Bobo are constantly on the phone or getting emails and texts about evidence and sightings of Bigfoot. These guys, too, are consumed with it. They walk the walk and have for years. Somehow, we watch forty minutes (plus commercials), and we believe that we know them and how they are. But television doesn't let us see the whole story.

For instance, Matt Moneymaker comes across as crass and whiny on the show: that's how they play him. In reality, he is very bright and thoughtful. Sure, he has opinions, but he has been doing this stuff for a long time. He has developed a database that even his critics use. What does that say about the man?

Cliff Barackman is likeable and a sincerely good guy, someone you want to go in the woods with. And he has courage. Cliff will sleep by himself in a sleeping bag in the middle of a trail in a wilderness setting. I know very few people who will do that. He's open-minded and practical in his thinking, someone we can all relate to. Since the show, Cliff has opened the North American Bigfoot Museum in Boring, Oregon. He's also become one of the most respected in analyzing purported Bigfoot footprints and casts.

Cliff Barackman is as nice as anyone in the Bigfoot field. He is legitimately consumed with Bigfoot.

James "Bobo" Fay is one of those guys who is adamant in his beliefs and has a lot of experience to verify what he says. Everyone likes him, and he is kind to all. He is a big teddy bear of a guy. One of the best things Bobo did for me was convincing me to get a dog to go with me into the woods (Shade). He told me how one of his brief sightings occurred because he noticed his dog, Monkey, look in a direction, and Bobo looked too, and just for an instant he had a sighting.

Ranae Holland has always been kind to me. I have had breakfast with her a few times over the years and talked to her a lot on the ground when they are filming. She is a nice person and acknowledges things that she can't explain. She is kind in her objections to evidence, and that makes her hard to be upset with. On the conference tour Ranae is one of the most popular people whom people want to meet.

The Finding Bigfoot crew on one of their visits to West Virginia. From the left: Cliff Barackman, guest star Dr. Russell Jones, Matt Moneymaker, guest star Darren Pevarnik, James "Bobo" Fay, Ranae Holland

Let's be realistic: You can't sneak up on Bigfoot. Generally, they know when you are in a woods that they are in. You certainly can't sneak up on a Bigfoot when you have a television crew and everything that goes with that, including a big truck and catering! Sometimes the producers choose a location based on ease rather than what might be the best Bigfoot location.

The shows do their best, and they are sincere in wanting to find Bigfoot. However, they have to leave when the filming is over, regardless of the action. And they have to deal with many constraints during the filming. They have to go to the locations regardless of what the weather is doing. I think that the crew is doing the best it can under the circumstances. While it has been a great run and wildly successful by anyone's standards, I'm sure that if you ask the cast of *Finding Bigfoot*, there are changes they can recommend that would make the show better.

"Catching a snack" a Sybilla Irwin illustration representing my "treat food" theory

COLLECTION OF
PHOTOGRAPHS

Tree breaks can be evidence of Bigfoot, diseased trees, or snow
load. Always check the break for hair

Leaving toys, marbles, rocks, Nutella, peanut butter, etc. is an
interesting way to attract a primates curiosity

I was lucky to be back with my friends from Finding Bigfoot to do
a special episode

Shade. Some are leery of having a dog in the woods with them but they see and smell much that we don't. Spend enough time with them in the woods and you will notice

Otter Creek Wilderness Area. Possible Bigfoot track. Please don't go to these areas screaming and beating do it

Here is a garage sized bone dry area with a 10 foot ceiling. The way its sloped the water never goes in. In a remote area its hard to imagine a Bigfoot not being in here at some point. eDNA testing for Bigfoot may yield results if it was recent enough

Its hard to tell from the pic but it's a leaf bed and has a few turkey feathers in and around it. I've found large leaf beds several times under rock overhangs

Low tech attempt to get Bigfoot hair. Bacon grease smeared at 8 feet around the tree. Packing tape reversed in sections. Easier in areas without a lot of bears

After what I belief a brief encounter with a Bigfoot, I carry a GoPro on my hiking staff every single time I'm in the woods

It's common for me to leave baby food jars in prominent places just trying to stimulate curiosity. Only in remote areas. I use different colors to see if one may work best. Some have cameras on them, and others don't

I have no idea if a Bigfoot did this, but it's not natural. About 50 yards from a right-of-way, and near a tree break make it interesting

Many will look at this picture and say that your not supposed to go down this path. Learn ecology and study ecosystems. These are elm trees and most likely died of Dutch Elm disease

Cemeteries, much like rights-of-way, create an edge for wildlife and are often close to woods

Cliffs and rock faces give security to primates. A south facing one is even better, providing warmth in cooler times of the year

Clearcuts are not of much use to animals for food for about ten years but I believe that Bigfoot may use them for cover and security in areas that there aren't expansive forests

While I believe tree manipulation is vastly overstated in the Bigfoot field there are instances that are compelling. Notice the tree being woven in and out. Photo courtesy of Ronie Powell

I call much of this "tree litter." While some find meaning, I find them all over the woods. While Bigfoot may make them no one has seen one make one

Tracks found with dermatoglyphics are compelling. Found in a forest in winter even more so. Dermatoglyphics are essentially fingerprints, here found on the foot

Track found by witness after sighting. I met with witness one week later and found a fresh track. Six miles from West Virginia the state capital

What in nature, deep in a clear cut, carries broken berry canes to a stump?

Clear footprints are hard to come by in Appalachia. I believe Bigfoot to be cognizant of not leaving footprints

Tracks found in a bottom in remote Kanawha County will often
show details even if full of water when cast

West Virginia really does live up to its billing as "the Pacific
Northwest of the east"

Pheromone chips may prove to be effective in baiting. I've used them with camera traps

This log was lifted and not rolled. I was in this same area at the same time 5 years in a row because of suspected Bigfoot activity at that time

PART THREE
WEST VIRGINIA, BIGFOOT'S MOUNTAIN HOME

This part of the book was perhaps the most fun to write. I am presenting evidence and my conclusions about the future of Bigfoot, or, as some say, Bigfootery. I believe the search for Bigfoot is serious and has serious implications for science, society, and history. Here I am trying to bring together all the fieldwork done in West Virginia and Ohio, which indicates to me that, indeed, there may well be a reproducing population of Bigfoot living in Appalachia.

And I must admit, I can't resist an opportunity to tell others about the Mountain State, the beautiful place where I live. In fact, the one request that I made of the producers of *Finding Bigfoot* was to "make West Virginia look special and show its beauty." Many people have told me the West Virginia episodes were not only some of the best but also some of the most scenic of the series.

Consider the evidence, enjoy the tour, and then come to your own conclusions.

Map of West Virginia showing major cities

CHAPTER 8
YAHOOS

MILES AND MILES OF REMOTE FORESTLAND

Most people's perception is that Bigfoot sightings started in 1967 with the Patterson-Gimlin film. You know the one, Bigfoot cruising along with big arm swings and looking back at the camera. Patty, as she is called, on the sand bar in northern California. After many and repeated attempts to label it a hoax, the P-G film has never been disproven and remains some of the best video evidence out there. However, in actuality, stories of hairy or wild men in the woods originated centuries before that film. Reports on North American sightings go back hundreds of years.

Native American tribes have numerous names for Bigfoot. Some people believe the name Sasquatch came from a word for the creature used by a tribe that lives around Vancouver, BC, called the sa'sq'ets. Others believe Sasquatch is a hybridization of Native American or First People's words or the result of a translation error. Most researchers refer to either Bigfoot or Sasquatch. Scientists seem to prefer Sasquatch, as Bigfoot seems more of a pop culture name. There are many names of Bigfoot-like creatures around the globe, each one based on some appropriate name for that particular culture. I won't address those creatures in this book except in passing. I really don't have a preference one way or another as to what a Bigfoot or Sasquatch is called; I just want to see the species recognized and am interested in knowing more about it.

In West Virginia the most recent of the Native American tribes are the Shawnee, Delaware, Cherokee, and Iroquois. They all lived in West Virginia, sometimes at the same time, generally along the edges of the state. West Virginia was a hunting ground for the tribes. The Iroquois tried to control West Virginia for the trade routes and depending on the time in history, were a band of either five or six tribes. At least two had names for Bigfoot. The Iroquois in general used the name "Ot-ne-yar-hed," which translated to "stonish giant." The Seneca sect of the Iroquois used the name "Ge-Gno'sqwa," which translated to "stone-coat." I have no idea what "stone" refers to in the names, maybe because they could be found on rock tops, or maybe it has to do with camouflage, or hides so tough it could deflect arrows. The Cherokee nation used the name "Kecleh-kudleh," meaning "hairy savage."

In terms of print, the oldest Bigfoot report I was able to locate in West Virginia was in Bluefield in 1895. That particular one refers to a "wild man," which is how Bigfoot was often referred to in historical times. Most of the states around West Virginia, all part of Appalachia, have reports going back to the 1800s. The earliest wild man reference I found was an 1820 newspaper report from Pennsylvania. As one would expect, the number of reports increased with advances in technology. There have been reports fairly consistently in print up to more modern times.

In terms of expeditions, the BFRO led some of the earliest, those being in the mid-'90s. Largely taking place in the high-mountain counties, the earliest expeditions represented a phase of pre-technology research. I call it that because though there had been outings and research for decades, by and large they were carried out with traditional hunting tools like tracking, binoculars, and various animal calls.

Probably the earliest use of advanced technology for Bigfoot research happened in the 1970s. Then, as noted, Ron Morehead and Al Berry recorded purported Bigfoot sounds in the California Sierra Nevada Mountains, which, in recent years, were labeled language by noted linguist Scott Nelson. Since the Sierra Sound recordings, several groups have made their way to West Virginia for high-tech research. All of the BFRO expeditions are now technology based and include the use of thermal imagers, drones, night-vision devices, modern audio recorders, and other high-tech tools.

The newest national park, the New River Gorge National Park in south-central West Virginia is one of the best Bigfoot habitats in the state

YAHOOS IN THE MOUNTAIN STATE

Early pioneers in West Virginia, and really throughout Appalachia, often referred to Bigfoot as the Yahoo. I have heard that the reason for the name was that Bigfoot made a sound that sounded like yahoo. I believe it may have come from Jonathan Swift's 1726 book, *Gulliver's Travels*. The book was very popular with early pioneers and describes a large, hairy animal that smells horrible. In discussions that he had before his death, it was reported that Daniel Boone, who lived in both West Virginia and nearby Kentucky, regretted that he had shot a yahoo. In fact, in eastern Kentucky, in the Daniel Boone National Forest, there is a Yahoo Falls.

The West Virginia counties with the most Bigfoot reports are Pendleton, Pocahontas, and Randolph, which are in the eastern mountains. These counties, which are connected to each other, are mountainous and isolated. Farms in the bottoms of the hollows have large tracts of wilderness surrounding them. Also, these remote counties have small populations. They have large deer populations, orchards, crops, silage, and plentiful precipitation.

I think it is most striking that the state's counties with the smallest human populations have the highest number of Bigfoot sightings. According to reports, Bigfoot sightings are most common in the summer and fall. In all likelihood that is when the most people are outside and have an opportunity for a sighting. In addition, about half of the sightings are at night, leading one to believe that if humans are less active at night yet half the sightings are then, Bigfoot is probably more active at night.

Looking at the numbers of reports and knowing the state as I do, I believe that there are large Bigfoot populations in these counties, possibly more than a family group per county. And, of course, in nature's way to spread the gene pool, there are probably transient males striding through these counties.

I believe that there are counties in West Virginia that may have higher populations of Bigfoot but contain so much federal land and so few people that there are not as many reported sightings. One such area is the Cranberry Wilderness Area, roughly in the center of the Monongahela National Forest in the east-central portion of the state.

When I look at West Virginia and its fifty-five counties, I estimate roughly one family group of Bigfoot per county. I say this based on the number of reports and my experience, an educated guess if you will. Some of the larger and more remote counties may have more. So my

Bigfoot population estimate for the state is around 200–225 Bigfoot. The BFRO Bigfoot estimating method is to divide the number of bears by 68, which would put their group's estimate at 250.

In contrast, Dr. Grover Krantz, the physical anthropologist, estimated that there is one Bigfoot per 100 bears, which would mean that around 170 Bigfoot live in West Virginia. Dr. Krantz was talking specifically about the Pacific Northwest, so his estimate may not be as useful in West Virginia. While these methods are interesting and helpful for estimates, each area or region must be looked at individually.

One might think that if there were that many Bigfoot, surely more people would have seen one. But out of the seventeen thousand bears in West Virginia, how many are seen in the wild? Most people still haven't seen one, and the great majority who have seen one have been in a car. A bear's sense of smell is great, but they can't see well, so it's certainly easier to come upon one upwind than a creature that has the ability to see well.

While seemingly fairly curious about humans, Bigfoot are wary of being in an area of human presence. For example, have you ever lost your dog? I have many times when coon and rabbit hunting with dogs. Lost dogs are hard to find even when fairly close to the house and they aren't trying to hide from you. Imagine how much harder it would be to find an animal deep in the woods that is intensely private and has the brain of a primate. One can assume Bigfoot has been in a given area for generations and has learned where people are or are not at different times of the year.

ON STORIES, PHOTOS AND RECORDINGS

Two stories remind me the most of this fact. Due to leaf litter and rocks, West Virginia is generally not a good place to find tracks. Keep in mind that there seems to be evidence that chimpanzees and mountain lions seem to be cognizant of the danger of leaving their tracks and try in many cases to avoid leaving them. I think it's safe to assume that Bigfoot would be hesitant or leery of leaving their tracks.

I took a story in Greenbrier County where two gentlemen saw a Bigfoot running. When the Bigfoot came to a "fresh" logging road, rather than just running across the road, it jumped it, apparently in an effort to not leave tracks. I mean think about that, it's scared and running from the humans it just saw but by reflex jumps the road. I also took a report from a gentleman who was working on a dozer that had broken down in a remote location. Two witnesses observed a Bigfoot watching the man work on his dozer. Although a couple of hundred yards away from the dozer in the forest, the Bigfoot was "peeking" warily around a tree to watch!

Except for the game cam photo given to me by Matt Rogers taken in northeast West Virginia, there is really not much video footage from the state. And to be truthful, while Matt's photo is compelling, especially given his prior game cam photographs and nearby sightings, it is inconclusive.

Some controversial photos exist here and there, but I don't know the photographers personally, so I can't speak to the veracity of the photos. On YouTube you can find "The Snowshoe WV Bigfoot." Though intriguing, no one can track down the individual who posted it. That same Snowshoe area, which is so popular with skiers, comes close to backing up to the Cranberry Wilderness Area that I have spoken about.

To give you an idea of the remoteness of the Cranberry Wilderness Area, several years ago a National Guard helicopter crashed there. For rescuers to get to the helicopter, they had to use borrowed snowcats, travel for three hours on an abandoned railroad grade, and then hike an additional three hours to reach the site. Amazing! The rescue team had to travel for six hours through rugged terrain, on an off-road vehicle and foot, and they knew the object of their search and where it was located!

Many audio recordings have come out of West Virginia. My good friend and BFRO investigator Darren Pevarnik and I have organized several expeditions in the state, during which many of the participants have made quality recordings. In addition, the BFRO's main audio investigator, who goes by the moniker Monongahela, has made many recordings in West Virginia. Do an internet search, and he will even show you how to make a long-duration recorder.

A long-duration recorder is a recorder with an added battery capacity that is placed in the woods. It turns on around dusk and shuts off around daylight. It can record for around six weeks. By placing a few different recorders around a general area, it's possible to figure out the direction that most of the possible Bigfoot sounds may be coming from and where they may be staying. You could almost triangulate the Bigfoot sounds if you have enough recorders in place.

Monongahela has a place in West Virginia he regards as his personal research area. He speaks at many events for the group as well as podcasts, educating others about the possible calls a Bigfoot may make and how to recognize them. Monongahela is a military-trained crypto analyst who works in the defense industry and for that reason keeps his identity concealed in public forums. We also have an investigator in Michigan named Jim Sherman who does audio work. Jim is a teacher who is "ate up" with Bigfoot. You can find his work and podcast online. If you met these guys, you would be very impressed. Not only are they genuinely nice, but they are as sharp as tacks!

Steep hillsides and hidden springs and hollows are a hallmark of West Virginia

West Virginia, with its vast expanses of wilderness, is one of the few places that you can go and get away from everyone. It's still possible to go to many areas where no one has tried to research or locate a Bigfoot. I have talked to many people who either come to West Virginia or have a place in the state just for the purpose of Bigfoot research. I think there is a good chance that some of the best evidence to come out may come from West Virginia.

The ancestors of any Bigfoot that calls West Virginia home would have originally crossed the Bering Land Bridge between Asia and North America. The bridge was open ten to twenty thousand years ago. I speculate that Bigfoot would have then migrated south and east to West Virginia, searching for home territories and following game.

ALMOST HEAVEN, WEST VIRGINIA

Part of what makes West Virginia such a great place for a possible documented primate is its uniqueness. Many call West Virginia the "Pacific Northwest of the East Coast." The Pacific Northwest is the undisputed king of Bigfoot sightings and activity, so that puts West Virginia in good company.

West Virginia is the only state entirely in the Appalachian Mountains, with its highest mountain, Spruce Knob, at around 5,000 feet. Its lowest elevation is Harpers Ferry at 240 feet. Mean elevation is around 1,500 feet, which is the highest of any state east of the Mississippi. Reviews nationally of many of the sightings show that much of the Bigfoot activity is at around 1,500–2,000 feet. The elevation in West Virginia increases from west to east at the Allegheny Plateau, where the rugged country can receive as much as seventy inches of rain. Generally, the higher the precipitation, the larger the Bigfoot population. In West Virginia, the counties with the highest precipitation are some of the least populated in the eastern United States. That's good for Bigfoot territory but terrible for sighting reports because there are so few people in the area to actually see a Bigfoot! Ironically, in eastern West Virginia, the two least populated counties, Pendleton and Pocahontas, are very high on the list for reported sightings. This makes me think that they have relatively high Bigfoot populations.

Temperature can vary greatly in West Virginia, primarily due to elevation. For instance Snowshoe or Canaan Valley, both of which average around 4,000 feet in elevation, can average two hundred inches of snow a year. Charleston, while still steep and hilly, is in the lowlands and gets only around thirty-six inches of snow or less annually. In general, we who live here expect there to be at least a ten-degree difference when we travel to the mountains. So in less than an hour drive, you can see huge differences in weather and conditions. The general rule of thumb is that for every thousand feet of gain in elevation, the temperature is what you would expect about two hundred miles farther north in the United States.

Elevation and temperature bring up the topic of whether or not Bigfoot migrate. Certainly, if they do, West Virginia would be a prime location to witness this migration. My own belief is that they generally have a territory that they may stay in with possibly the exception in regard to mating, which may cause some travel. If I had to guess how large territories are, mine would be a guess of 250 square miles on average. I would suspect it to be larger out west. That seems like a reasonable number for a large, relatively smart omnivore. Where they are in that area is based on the time of year, such as different food availabilities, hunting seasons, and weather among other factors. I tell witnesses that if they find tracks, have a sighting, or hear a suspected Bigfoot vocal, there is a chance the animal could be in the same general area at the same time next year.

BIGFOOT POPULATION

With one of the lowest numbers of people per square mile in the eastern United States, West Virginia has plenty of room for the Bigfoot to roam. The land itself is also breathtaking. Drive through West Virginia on one of the main interstates, I-77, I-64, I-79, and the steep rugged terrain is impressive, with much of it seemingly inaccessible. However, this same mountainous terrain and the hollows within it can limit sightings. While connectivity is improving, internet and cell service can be spotty at best in the mountains, also limiting the "get up here now" sort of calls. Aside from all of that, West Virginia is still thirteenth in the number of sightings nationally.

Waterways and rights-of-way are both believed to be pathways that a Bigfoot may follow, and West Virginia is loaded with them. Because West Virginia produces so much energy, these rights-of-way are plentiful from our coal-fired power plants to the entire East Coast. The rugged hills are loaded with springs and seeps, which provide a lot of pure, healthy drinking water, so Bigfoot wouldn't even have to visit the creeks and rivers of the valleys and bottomlands.

In West Virginia about 16% of the land is owned by the federal or state government and is basically unpopulated. The population of the state is about 1.8 million people and dropping. The whole state is about equal to the population of either Philadelphia or San Diego.

About 20% of West Virginia's population lives on the I-64 corridor, the forty miles between Charleston and Huntington in the west-central part of the state. A good portion of the rest of West Virginia's population lives in the northeast panhandle of the state, which is considered part of the greater Washington, DC, metropolitan area. So clearly, the remainder of the state, the five hours between those places, is lightly populated. Many counties in West Virginia have only around ten people per square mile.

And it is said that if West Virginia's hilly and mountainous terrain were to be flattened out, it would cover as much territory as almost the entire territory of the United States. Flying out of Charleston's Yeager Airport, the largest in the state, the vastness of the green canopy is shocking. Spreading in all directions as far as the eye can see.

While all of West Virginia is considered remote, the most remote section is the Cranberry Wilderness Area in the roughly million acres of the Monongahela National Forest. Among the several designated wilderness areas, you can hike for many miles straight up and down before finding the narrowest of forest roads.

One of the things that is so hard to visualize is the actual variety of the terrain. For instance, in the Cranberry Wilderness Area there are rugged, lush valleys and woodlands thick with rhododendrons. In terms of the thickness of plants and trees, the wilderness looks like a tropical rain forest. So it's easy to imagine a Bigfoot standing in the tangle, looking right at you, and you never suspecting it, let alone seeing it.

When leaves are still on the trees, it's hard to see far off the sparse, unmarked trails, which are few and far between. Cell service? Yeah, you can walk the twenty miles to find it. Recently, a wilderness expert was lost in the area and never found even after a search by a hundred people and dogs. He's just one to have gone missing. One April, I was lost four or five times on the same trip, and it was one of the only times I have felt fear in the woods.

The New River Gorge area, which is our newest national park, is so steep that pictures cannot adequately depict it. I was recently hiking in the gorge to a cliff that I had recently heard wood knocks come from, and it took two hours to get to the base of the cliff, which on a straight line was less than a quarter mile. Rocky and full of snakes that make many outdoorsmen wait till winter to venture off trail. There is safety there for a Bigfoot. It can sit high and look over the terrain below with no easy way for anything to get near it.

Author in a mine vent in Fayette County in remote south-central West Virginia. These may be used similarly to a cave or rock overhang, and often located remotely. I found this one after hearing a wood knock and investigating

Interestingly, I found an eight-foot-tall vent pipe near where I had found a possible Bigfoot track and heard wood knocks, extending a quarter mile into a mountain, with nice warm air gushing out of it. Finding a large vent pipe is not uncommon; there are many such mine access points, drainpipes, etc., that are scattered all over the state, unblocked and hidden from view. It's easy to imagine a family of Bigfoot holing up in one of these during inclement weather. It is accepted that sixty feet into a mine or cave opening, the temperature stays a fairly consistent 58 degrees but can be even warmer deeper in a cave or mine. Regarding our barefooted friends, since they don't use light, they probably don't venture that far in.

Other areas like the lowlands and plateaus have flat farmland backed up to the hills. This gives a wide variety of plant and animal sources in the bottoms. A Bigfoot can sit up on the hills and watch deer eat in the fields and plot his or her hunt or wait for darkness to descend upon the fields to see what food may be there.

These steep mountainsides that go miles to the next road allow for security and kleptoparasitism of nearby properties and farms

CHAPTER 9
GEAR

When I go into the woods, my backpack is full of things I carry, such as supplies and snacks. Every hiker, Bigfooter, or outdoorsman prefers particular supplies and foods, based on their experience or lack thereof. Over the years I have found that when I go in the woods bigfooting, certain items are handy or necessary. Here I want to give the readers my insight on the must-have "toys" for a Bigfoot outing.

THERMAL IMAGER

Thermals show a heat source, and there are a number of brands in the marketplace. It used to be mainly the brand Flir, so we would commonly call a thermal a Flir, but now several quality brands are out there. The device is for sighting a heat signature and capturing it in a picture or a video. A thermal is able to see a long distance, quality and distance is based on price point, but limited in a thicket or heavy cover. A Bigfoot needs to be close to be definitive in a thermal, as it's just too difficult to discern shape, clothes, and size from a distance.

Thermals used to be exceptionally expensive, but the technology has gotten less expensive over the years. The thermal used on *Finding Bigfoot* cost around $30,000, obviously too expensive for most people. I use a Flir Scout, which cost me around $4,000, but I am currently looking at the Pulsar Helion 2 XP50 Pro 2.5-20 thermal. While it's at the same price point, the technology is eight years newer and is much improved over my Flir. Thermals at this price point have good resolution and can record on an SD card. SD (secure digital) is a memory card used in portable devices (game cameras as well), which is about the size of a postage stamp. Thermal imagers are all about the resolution: 640 x 480 ppi is what you are after (or better). Lower resolution models that are out at about $500 produce images that are too fuzzy to examine details, and higher resolution models require an enormous amount of memory in the device and thus increase the price.

Even Matt Moneymaker from Finding Bigfoot can't resist Shade

A word of advice about using thermals. When you see something in it, DO NOT look away. I can't tell you the number of times a researcher sees something, looks away, and the figure disappears! This advice goes with daytime visual sightings as well. If you see a Bigfoot or think that you do, NEVER look away regardless of what is happening around you. It's common for other Bigfoot to attempt to distract you for an easy escape by the previously spotted one. They may scream, break branches, throw things at you, any number of things to distract an intruding human.

NIGHT VISION

The best available to the public right now is Gen 3. Each time there is an improvement in this technology, they call it a new generation (Gen). The very first night vision was Gen 1. It can give off a greenish or whitish glow depending upon the type that you have. You can see exceptionally well, but imagine what the military has! When buying, you have to make sure that the optics and tube are of good quality. Brand names and origins change constantly, so make sure to do a little research to know what companies are producing quality optics at that time. If you get a Gen 3 tube with poor optics, you'll get a better price but won't be satisfied. I don't use one yet but will for sure when it's possible to record on an SD card in the unit rather than have to wire some contraption together to be able to record. For something good, I would expect to pay $6,000 to $7,000. I think the ideal situation is to have a couple of people together with both thermal and night vision in the woods at the same time.

GAME CAMERA

This is my research wheelhouse, as I have over forty game cameras in the field. You need both a cheap and an expensive model. You can set up the cheap camera as bait, or if someone is feeding a suspected Bigfoot, they can put out the cheap game camera to see if the animal quits coming in. Bigfoot has a history of somehow avoiding game cameras, or it could be that Bigfoot are just so rare. I believe it reasonable to assume that if I put a very cheap game camera out, Bigfoot would surely hear or recognize it and stop coming in, although a coon or possum wouldn't care about the game camera being in place. If it's something other than a Bigfoot, you get a picture of what is coming in, and if it's a Bigfoot, the taking of food will stop because they are avoiding the area. If that happens, then take the camera down and see if the feeding starts once again. I have seen this happen a number of times. On a number of occasions, sticks have been thrown at a cheap camera.

For the cheap camera, I use a Bushnell camera because it's small and inexpensive, but I have witnesses go to Walmart and buy the cheapest one. For the expensive cameras, I am partial to Reconyx. The Reconyx brand is the quietest and has the fastest trigger speed. It also shows no red at flash. The recent models have the ability to turn off the infrared flash if you suspect that is an issue in getting Bigfoot pictures.The battery life is well over a year with lithium batteries. The "louder" the camera, the shorter the battery life in general. Across the nation there is not a consensus, and investigators are trying whatever brand they want to.

Since the first edition, a number of studies have come out regarding game cameras. I have become more convinced than ever that the Bigfoot may hear the game cameras. Most are at least thirty decibels, and small children can usually hear them. Many researchers believe that Bigfoot can see in the infrared spectrum, which the flash of game cameras and night vision use (it's optional to use). In game cameras the infrared is only used during the flash, so unless a Bigfoot would see a flash of a picture being taken, it wouldn't know the camera was there. Many have turned off the flash or disabled it and still don't have Bigfoot pictures to show, further reinforcing that it may be a noise issue that we are dealing with. Further, even with no-flash game cameras, many animals are still looking at the camera, indicating they may have heard a sound.

So many want a picture of Bigfoot on their game camera, and heaven knows that I do too, but we may overlook other purposes. When in place for a while, we begin to note how many deer, coyotes, bobcats, etc. are in that area. I have noticed that many times I will have a week or so that I will have all the normal animals disappear or not be as frequent. I hypothesize that there is something altering the normal wildlife patterns, and we should consider this. Does that mean that it's a Bigfoot? No, it could be any number of things, but it's worth noting and keeping track of. I try to be in that particular woods during that particular time to look around.

I also believe that we can use the game cameras, even if heard, to shape the Bigfoot movement in the area. By that I mean blocking certain courses or paths with cameras and shifting that movement toward a better camera setup or trap. For instance, maybe a portion of a creek or waterway that emits enough noise that it may block the camera's noise and allow the desired picture of an animal that went that way to avoid the other game cameras.

In the end, because of the rarity of the creature, it's hard to know if your setup was not good or a Bigfoot just didn't come through or within fifty feet of a game camera.

A rare fresh track in the Appalachian soil. The great majority of the time the Bigfoot seem to walk around or it would be covered with leaf litter

I had a witness recently who was a skilled woodsman and, after a close daylight encounter, became intrigued by the Bigfoot subject. He sent me a picture of an area, telling me a certain portion was perfect for Bigfoot to move through. I told him in my years of doing research and studying maps that I had found that there were many more "perfect" Bigfoot locations than there were Bigfoot. The animal is rare and not everywhere.

HANDHELD RECORDER

In the BFRO we joke all the time, for good reason, about remembering to turn on our recorders before we even get out of the vehicles. There are literally dozens of stories about there being a wood knock or vocalization as soon as someone gets out of their vehicle and hasn't had a chance to turn on their recorder.

In fact, when I was hosting the *Finding Bigfoot* television show for their recent reunion celebrating their original ten seasons, we heard a scream while eating dinner before we even went in the woods. Of course, no one had a recorder going. It's important to have one so that you can document the when, what, and where, and at some point, maybe a scientist or researcher may be looking at your information. You are keeping track of all this stuff you come across in the woods, right?

At present the researcher-recommended recorders are the Olympus WS-853 and the Sony PCM-M10, but the Sony is very hard to find. You might try using a quality external microphone to help with quality. At the end of the day, any type of recorder is better than not having one.

RED LIGHT

Everyone must have one. They don't ruin your night vision, and it allows you to get into the woods somewhat stealthily. It's really funny that as you spend more time in the woods, you are constantly looking for a brighter red light! Choose carefully though: you also want a light that doesn't make you flip through all of the white light settings to get to the red light. In dark woods at night, even a brief flash of white light can make it hard to see for a while and is visible for a very long distance.

You can get a fairly decent one on Amazon by looking for red light hunting headbands. Most of the others are so dim that it can be dangerous in the woods and hard to see snakes if it's that time of year. For the brightest, which is also dimmable, I like the Noxx Dagger X headlamp available at noxxflashlights.com. I have used these exclusively for a very long time.

Admittedly, when you are in a sensitive area, you may want to turn the brightness down, but for getting in and out of the woods with a red light, the Noxx can't be beat. I also want to mention that I carry a very bright white LED light in my back pocket or backpack. If I get in an area where there is mud or where I may be able to find a track, like a pond or stream bank, and I am just walking and not concerned about being stealthy, I will turn on the LED light to investigate a track better. If there is an injury to someone with you or you need to be seen, you need to have a white headlamp or flashlight on you as well. And one last thing: it is a must to carry backup batteries with you, and not ones that have lain in your pack for a year.

Let me just say that you should carry with you whatever is going to make you feel ok if you have to spend the night in the woods because of an injury or whatever reason.

WOOD KNOCKER

I know that a lot of people yell and scream supposed Bigfoot sounds, but I think it's simpler to be unobtrusive and do OCCASIONAL wood knocks as a locator tool. Researchers use all types of objects they believe work best. I use two to three measured knocks on the rare times that I do any. I usually use a walking stick that I am carrying or a Latin percussion jam block (I got the jam block idea from my friend, California researcher Bart Cutino) medium pitch, red, found on Amazon for $34. Some investigators in the Pacific Northwest use a fish club.

GPS

Who wants to get lost in the woods? I can't tell you the number of times that I didn't know exactly where I was in the woods. Sure, I think it's a great idea to be proficient with a compass. I think it's a good idea to know the major waterways in the area you are hiking. Before you go into the woods, check your map and locate the borders of the woods on each compass heading. Also recognize which is the quickest way out of the woods. I remember a kid here in West Virginia who was deer hunting and got turned around and, like most, was told to go downhill until you find a road or creek to follow. He found civilization but had to get someone to drive him the fifty miles back to the camping spot.

I have an iPhone and use the apps on it. There are apps and GPS on your phone that do not require cell service but rather use satellites. There are many good ones, but I use OnX exclusively. Many times, gas well roads and trail names will even show up. I carry a backup lipstick charger for my phone.

So for everyday hikes, it goes like this. I know the closest roads or borders in all directions. I have learned to be proficient at telling the cardinal directions by sun, moon, and trees, etc. I use my iPhone with the OnX app to chart my hike and see where I am. I use the Apple Ultra watch to mark my start location, and it can point me back to it at any time if something were to happen to my phone.

BINOCULARS

To truly enjoy a Bigfooting expedition or the wild outdoors in general, I strongly recommend bringing along a good set of binoculars. If you are not used to using binoculars, the general rule for the first pair is that smaller is better. Compact binoculars are easy to carry and quick to use. If your binoculars feel large to you, I recommend purchasing a binocular window mount or a hiking staff with a binocular screw adaptor to steady them for long-range viewing. The screw on the hiking staff will also fit your camera. My binoculars are in my vehicle all the time whether bigfooting or not.

Important: If you are buying binoculars for the first time, select low power on the small diameter wheels, 8x22. If you decide to buy a large binocular, select no more than 10x (i.e., 10x42 or 10x50). Do not buy 10x small binoculars, as they are difficult to stabilize and have limited eye relief.

As with many things, in binoculars you get what you pay for, although with the rise in internet sales, acceptable beginner quality can be found at reasonable prices. Finally, practice with your binoculars before going afield. Culminating barrels is easily learned by observing roof shingles, near and far.

GOPRO

Well, the GoPro wasn't in the first edition. After having what I believe to be a brief Bigfoot encounter, here it is. Had I been carrying my GoPro on my hiking staff like I do now, literally every trip in the woods, we would have more video evidence to talk about.

It's not a dead Bigfoot or even a piece of a body, but as my friend and *MonsterQuest* producer Doug Hajicek has told me, "Four seconds of fairly close, high-quality (4K) video, will be compelling and get a lot of people even more interested." I agree with him. Even though I'm out a couple of times a week year-round, I have yet to get another shot, but when I do, I will be ready.

For those not familiar with a GoPro or similar cameras, they are a small action camera that produces high-quality videos. They come with a myriad of attachments so you can put them on about any part of your body or even your dog. I have a handful of batteries and just change them out as I need to when I'm in the woods. It's not that practical to get our phone out in time to hope to record something. I have tried to get bears or large deer the last couple of years on mine, and it's hard to do. For every dozen videos showing cool wildlife captures, there are hundreds or thousands that were missed.

"The Perch" illustration by Sybilla Irwin representing the author's "perch" theory

CHAPTER 10
THE HUNT

"He who seeketh long enough and hard enough will find the truth, whatever that may be." Roger Patterson, Bigfoot researcher who filmed the 1967 Patterson-Gimlin Bigfoot footage in northwest California

GOING ON A BIGFOOT HUNT

People are all different. However, we behave in similar ways most of the time. Bigfoot, I believe, are likewise all different but also share certain characteristics and behaviors. Whole books have been written on supposed Bigfoot behavior, not to mention the existence of literally tens of thousands of reports and encounters that show their behavior. I'm not going to comment much on all that has already been said. Take time to read many of the BFRO Bigfoot reports, particularly the ones in your region, listen to the witnesses on podcasts such as mine (*Wide Open Research*), and they will provide insight to many of the behaviors of Bigfoot.

Some places, like Ohio for instance, only have so much area for a Bigfoot to be. I remember asking investigator Mark Maisel years ago, why bother to investigate Ohio when West Virginia was obviously a better state than Ohio in so many ways? His retort: "It's easier to fish and catch something in a pond than a lake." A lot of truth to that. My game cameras were so remote in West Virginia that I didn't see a person on one for eight years. In Ohio at almost any location, someone will go through in the course of a year.

With smaller spaces of green in some states, Bigfoot seem to get more comfortable with humans by necessity in those areas. In Ohio, at places like Salt Fork State Park, it's hard to trust anything that comes from there unless you know some of the hidden areas. People come from all over, hitting trees and screaming. It's not hard to imagine those people communicating with each other! Yelling Bigfoot screams and doing wood knocks back and forth!

West Virginia simply doesn't have that many people around, and many areas are very large and exhausting to explore in and around for Bigfoot. But if you do, I say you definitely can slow down the Bigfoot activity in an area. For instance, we did two expeditions at Blackwater State Park, plus I brought in the *Finding Bigfoot* television show for an episode there. Many of the people who went on the expedition kept returning on their own as well. Now, the park has their own Bigfoot-type related activities. In the immediate area, while I'm sure the Bigfoot are still around, the activity is no longer what it once was.

Initially, when investigator Darren Pevarnik and I started doing research in the area, it was much easier to get activity. Each time we were there, we might find or hear something indicative of Bigfoot activity. But now we no longer have "virgin" Bigfoot, so to speak. They have been educated. Are they there? Probably. They are quieter and more suspicious. They now pull back farther in the wilderness more quickly.

Recently, some audio came into the BFRO from a great spot where few people go. The individuals recording were doing wood knocks and other supposed Bigfoot sounds at night when they got a very loud and close response, followed by a large tree being broken. What did the individuals do? They turned on a white light, sounded an air horn, screamed, and then proceeded to run from the area. I don't believe that research helps Bigfoot research in any form.

In the beginning in a "fresh" area, and there are many more of those available in West Virginia than in most states, you can get more activity. Have a plan when you go in to capture evidence, as your activities will quickly educate them. They are bright and intelligent and will catch on quickly to what you are doing and may not be fooled a second time. I believe that most people are out there wanting an "experience" or an "encounter." They don't really have a plan of any type. Remember, your first shot, so to speak, in most cases, is going to be your best.

Remember that they have to want to come out and play. Well, many times in the Mountain State, or areas with deeper wilderness, they just withdraw. It's not central Ohio; in West Virginia and other areas of Appalachia, they have plenty of room to go where no one goes. Hopefully, you have done your homework on why they may be in the area. When I am taking or reading reports, one of the first things that I ask myself is "What was a Bigfoot doing in that area? Why was it there?" Answer those questions, and you are on a roll. For if you can find a "special" area, then maybe you can really get into some action.

A "special" area may be special for a number of reasons. It is a place they like to stay; it's a place they feel safe, or maybe near a good food source. Maybe an older Bigfoot is in the area and not very mobile or able to move out of the area. So if you can get into one of these areas, then not only will they stay longer, but it's also possible you may even experience aggressive territorial behavior such as growling, bluff charging, throwing rocks, breaking sticks, pushing over trees, doing whatever it can to try to get you to leave the area. I think that's what happened when I was fishing with my uncle at the remote beaver dam. That Bigfoot had its honey hole or perfect secluded spot for shelter, security, and food, and I was messing things up.

Where is the most common place to see a Bigfoot in West Virginia? It's the same place as in any other state. Yes, of course, the correct answer is Bigfoot crossing a road. Many of the BFRO investigators are using the dashcam-type cameras on their car dashes to record all the time while they drive. Surely the odds of getting something are infinitesimal, but you will never get anything without trying. I know of five reported Bigfoot crossings of Interstate 64 within a couple of miles of the exit at Lewisburg. So apparently, if there is no option, they will cross an interstate.

I remember looking at a couple of those reports, trying to figure out why in the heck they were crossing at this location so frequently. I decided that if there are not that many of them in the first place, and they were being seen that frequently, they must really be crossing that area often. I found out there is a cave system near the interstate at the location and also a slaughterhouse very close. Caroline Curtis, the BFRO's sharp dispenser of reports, refers to cases as a "BUO," a Bigfoot of Unknown Origin. Funny comments like that from Caroline remind all of us how little we actually know about what Bigfoot are doing with their time.

Don't forget that they will jump a fresh logging road to avoid leaving a track but ironically will cross an interstate if they have to. They will mimic birds and other animals and, most scary, even people. Some in the woods have heard four-hundred-pound frogs and two-hundred-pound birds. It sounds close to what is being mimicked but not quite exactly right. Many people report having their names called. As if it's not scary enough to have an eight-foot, eight-hundred-pound creature loose in the woods, but it's running around calling your name!

Bigfoot are said to be great mimics, and I believe it completely. It's well accepted within the BFRO that Bigfoot will mimic animals. Imagine the looks on investigators' faces deep in the woods in the black of the night when a supposed bird whistles that sounds so big and deep it may be hundreds of pounds. Imagine being deep in the woods around no water and hearing a very deep ribbit from a supposed frog. Other common sounds are machinery running and doors closing. They have enough intelligence to communicate with one another and are cognizant of sharing their location. Later I will talk about a report where more communication was observed.

I believe that Bigfoot will stay still unless they believe that they have been seen. Ever watched a deer when a four-wheeler is coming? They move off the trail and hold still until the danger moves past. I have reports where a large Bigfoot would stand behind a small tree for an instant until it was spotted. They have their very own "ghillie" suit, like armed forces snipers use for camouflage, and are very hard to see when they are standing very still by a tree or a brush line. Most of the places they frequent can be very dark as well. The more reports that I take as time goes on, I become acutely aware of how patient they are when it comes to not moving. Also, when moving away from humans, they will commonly go from tree to tree.

Bigfoot will avoid game cams, motion lights, and infrared. There are a lot of studies done in the last few years regarding the "noise" that game cameras make. I have made Faraday boxes, imported different materials to cover and shield the cameras with all types of natural materials, used ploys like cutting out a tree to fit a camera and putting the bark back over, or overlaying native vines to hide the camera. We have also tried a wide variety of synthetic materials, trying to block some of the noise. Generally, the longer the battery life, the less noise a camera makes, once again.

Regardless, you will notice the animals are looking at the camera even when it is really hidden well. A study out of Georgia made note that there are many fewer pictures of alpha male coyotes. Apparently, they are very wary and leery of the cameras. If coyotes know cameras are up, then surely a Bigfoot is capable as well. Maybe if it's a juvenile or adolescent Bigfoot, we might stand a greater chance of getting a pic than of an adult. In the end, there just isn't that many game cameras out there, and most are set up for seeing deer and not well hidden. With so few Bigfoot and so much land, it's a daunting task.

I have had witnesses who thought they had a Bigfoot coming around their house or that they were feeding "something" but weren't sure what it was. I have suggested putting out a cheap game camera to see if the action stopped, as I have mentioned previously.

I have had cases where the Bigfoot wouldn't come to an area if there was any snow on the ground, apparently not wanting to leave footprints. On more than one occasion witnesses were scared of what they thought was a Bigfoot around the house, and the problem was instantly solved by a motion light. If, of course, by "resolved" one means that the light scared away whatever it was. Yes, there are people who call and are fearful of the Bigfoot and want to know how to keep them away from their house. They don't want us to come out and look around, they just want them gone. I would love to hear more of their stories!

Bigfoot is a primate, no more, no less, in my opinion. He is stealthy, smart, illusive, rare, curious, flighty, but still a primate. Inside the Bigfoot community we talk about the "woo"; woo is the sound that a ghost makes. So when someone talks about the paranormal attributes of Bigfoot, they are "woo" or talking about "woo." I don't believe that Bigfoot can magically appear or disappear. I don't believe they are from another dimension. I don't think that they "cloak" or in any way become invisible. Just because it's hard to find something or get good evidence doesn't make it magical.

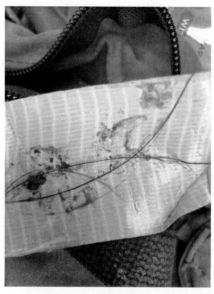

Collecting hair through hair traps and examining tree breaks may reward you with possible Bigfoot hair. This is boar hair that was later passed on to DNR and let them know they were in an area not formerly known. Another way to foster a good relationship with government employees

In the past I have talked to my friend and noted researcher Thom Powell, author of the great book *The Locals*, about the paranormal characteristics for some of the reports and sightings that he investigates. Like him, I believe that we may need to investigate some of the components of those claims. I believe it's imperative to report the "whole" encounter that someone experiences even if we can't explain all of it.

YOU WANT TO EXPERIENCE BIGFOOT. WHERE DO YOU START?

You have studied books, listened to podcasts, and visited responsible websites. You have built up vacation time and stashed away some dollars to do what? Attempt to encounter Bigfoot in its habitat. In West Virginia, habitat means mountains, so let's look at the general picture of what might confront you, and why.

The topics that follow are not speculative; they were learned through hard, long mountaineering experiences. In this section we will briefly discuss the where and why of a field investigation, not techniques to use. Techniques come later.

Briefly and specifically, this section answers the question: "If I am going to a Bigfoot zone where I have not been before, what am I looking for?" In that regard, this chapter surely applies to anywhere Bigfoot walks, be that in the Pacific coast mountains, the glacially flattened land of the Midwest, or southeastern US swamps.

THE "HALIBUT EFFECT"

Generally speaking, if an area has a history of wildlife sightings, whether it's a large halibut, a big buck, or a Bigfoot, if that area stays as it has been in the past, there is a good chance you can go back in the future and get action. The one difference with Bigfoot is that education of the public has changed research in some ways.

In turkey hunting we sometimes run across a turkey that is "call shy." A call shy turkey is one that has been educated on calls, decoys, etc. One time that turkey was in an area, heard a call, and went to the sound only to be scared by a human. He knows that it's not another turkey making calls but rather something that he fears and is dangerous. He becomes very fearful of coming to calls and only comes in pensively.

Nowadays, with Bigfoot, many times when you are in the woods doing research or on an expedition, you make some calls and get short, quick action, or an answer, and all is then quiet. What happened? You got busted! Usually, the Bigfoot will quietly slip back into the night. "They have to want to come out and play, or it doesn't matter."

I would start by going through the BFRO database at BFRO.net and find a place with a history of activity near you. If you find an area but are suspicious that it receives too much attention, or as Matt Money-maker says, "has been fished out," move to a location close to the "overfished" area that receives much less attention. Maybe try to go at a time of the year when not as many people will be around, like during the week or when the weather is cooler. The exception is if you believe the Bigfoot are "dumpster diving" or sorting through trash cans, then you need to be there when there are people there. Look for a way into the park that comes from a relatively remote region with limited human access.

Finding a beaver pond with fish is a good way to sit and listen and hope that the area Bigfoot may become interested in you

WATER

Remember the words from the immortal Bigfoot film *The Legend of Boggy Creek*: "They always follow the water." Just like most animals, Bigfoot really do all head for water eventually. While I believe that they lay up or rest on hillsides or higher ground, they are commonly found around the water. They require water, and many of their food sources drink the same water. Food opportunities may present themselves at the water, whether it's catching salmon like bears do, or just watching for deer coming to drink. An added benefit is an increase in the diversity of plant foods that are found around water sources. If you are in a drought situation, look for areas that hold water regardless of how little rain an area is getting. Think about out-of-the-way sources of water. As Oregon field researcher Steven Kiley reminds us, "Everything loves beaver ponds."

As I write this, it's October and has been dry the last six weeks. Many of the small or ephemeral streams are dry where something hidden may want to drink. I will go out in a couple of days like normal and have already been thinking about where I can find water that still has privacy and cover.

FOOD/TREAT FOOD

Food is the great motivator of all primates. Bigfoot is a large animal and requires a lot of calories. That by itself might be a good argument for Bigfoot to move to lower elevations, which in West Virginia can be found quickly due to the steepness and the easy travel corridors. Ironically, a couple of the best reports in West Virginia have come from high altitudes in the winter, so maybe they aren't as susceptible to the cold as we think, or don't look at it like we do.

I believe that deer are a mainstay in a Bigfoot diet, so they need to have a solid population of deer. Deer really don't help locate Bigfoot in West Virginia, as deer are plentiful everywhere. I really don't think Bigfoot's need of deer helps us get any closer to them, and that's what it's all about. I look for something that I call "treat food," instead of deer.

A treat food is a type of food that is not readily available at all times. It may either be seasonal or rarely found. A treat could come from a family who lives way out and has a huge garden, an old homestead's apple trees, or a person who throws scraps out, and many other things. One time I was with investigator Darren Pevarnik in a remote location when we found a beech tree loaded with nuts. There was an enormous flat rock (about three by four feet) with piles of nuts that had been smashed by smaller rocks. Know any animals in nature using tools to smash nuts for food in the mountains of West Virginia?

Other treat foods that I can think of right away include mushrooms, ramps, berries (many types), fruit trees, trash (human leftovers, trash cans, dumpsters), and gardens. If you find a fruit tree in an area that is loaded with fruit and overnight it disappears, that's suspicious and may be a treat food. Recently, I was on an expedition where we were looking at an old remote homestead. There was a large pear tree that was loaded from top to bottom, with dozens of pieces of fruit on the ground. Although I'm sure that Bigfoot would love to eat the pears, we didn't spend time at the location. I could see that they clearly weren't using that tree, because of so much of the fruit still being in place.

I reserve the right to acknowledge there are a million treat foods that I am forgetting, and that people will remind me of! The point being that deer are everywhere, and the treat foods are not. They will travel to get them, and part of their schedule may be to include these foods.

PERCHES

This is my own phrase and hypothesis. I have seen what I call perches many times, and they can really help reveal Bigfoot activity in an area quickly. You can get into a general area fairly easily, but this is a way to get more specific and local. Because of Bigfoot's inquisitive and secretive nature, not to mention the need for food, Bigfoot will frequent perches. For example, I have seen many perches that overlook fishing areas around a lake. Many times, a park road dead-ends near a lake and should be considered.

Investigating high ground near the dead-end roads for perches may prove fruitful, especially if there is access to that area from a remote region. Look roughly seventy to one hundred yards from a spot and search for where a Bigfoot may watch fishermen, partiers, couples, or whoever happens to be there. Maybe fishermen leave guts, scraps, or there may be a trash can there. From this perch they can also watch for humans coming into their area.

What a perch looks like. Signs like tracks, rock stacks, broken limbs, etc. overlooking an area like a dead-end road next to a lake where a trash can and fish guts are commonly found

I have been with investigator Brad Kennan of Ohio and Darren Pevarnik of West Virginia and used maps to locate possible places like this. Usually, you can drive there and look around and figure out where a "perch" will be if there is one in that area. You can sometimes find a small path, a crushed-down area, stacked rocks, small twigs and broken sticks in an area. Usually, perches are not right on a deer trail or a hiking trail, and they are always connected directly to a remote or isolated area.

We know Bigfoot is interested in watching campers in their campsites. Choose your campsite based on a "perch" you found or where one could be. You can tell from a topo map which parts of a lake or campground are most likely to have a perch. First, you must find those remote locations from which they can come to the perch, but from there you have to be able to get specific. For instance, in West Virginia's New River Gorge National Park, there are miles of cliffs and canyon walls. Would Bigfoot feel safe to hang out on top and be able to watch for danger? Sure, but how do you get specific when there are fifty miles of cliffs and rocks?

Get away from areas where there are just too many people. Look for a lake, pond, fishing hole, primitive camping spot, or campground with access to that area from a relatively remote area, and go take a look. Many of these will be seasonal, so keep that in mind. When you find that perch, you will already know the general area you suspect they are coming from (remember, from the remote area). Once I find a perch, I go deeper into the woods to what I call the "staging area." I borrow that term from deer hunting. A lot of bucks will not want to enter clearings and fields prior to dark, so they hang back in a safe brushy area to wait, and this is called a staging area.

I believe it all works something like this. A Bigfoot, or a family of Bigfoot, have a location they generally hang out in a remote or isolated spot. Very seldom do humans ever venture there for whatever reason. There is water nearby, but not necessarily a large body; it might be just a spring. As dark nears, they move from there to an area a little closer to their perch area. This gives them a little view to watch and listen and make sure everything is okay. This is the staging area.

Then they move on to the next staging area and so on until they reach their perch area. The number of staging areas depend on how much land there is around the area and how remote it is. Once you find a perch, it's actually pretty easy to backtrack and find subtle clues like the broken branches and twigs, bark peeling off trees because something's been standing behind them, tree twists, or possibly even some cleared leaves.

Keep in mind how rare these animals are. It's not like there is a perch at every park or national forest. Do your homework, and maybe you can get lucky!

COVER

You can't have a Bigfoot without a place for it to get away from humans. I mentioned earlier about the Pennsylvania study of hunter movement several years ago that showed only a tiny percentage of people venture more than a quarter mile from the nearest road or trail. Deer hunters don't want to drag a deer far, and they certainly don't want to drag one uphill. Hunters often creep slowly through the woods a few steps at a time, following the quietest path possible. Usually that means following a trail or an old logging road.

Rock overhangs are common in areas where there may even be no caves, can serve as a place to get minerals or get out of inclement weather

I often ask people about the last time they were farther than a quarter mile from the nearest road or trail, and I can assure you very few people are ever deep in the woods. Aside from hunting season, people are seldom in the woods. Occasionally, ginseng or mushroom hunters venture back in the woods, but they are generally very visible for both you and Bigfoot. In fact, in West Virginia many times it seems as though Bigfoot may initially show some interest in a person being in a remote section where they aren't used to seeing them. Many times, they will creep back farther into the woods, where there is plenty of room and places no human ever sees. Citizens in populated states think that people are everywhere, and all of it has been explored. People in West Virginia know that there is plenty of room, and there are many places that not a soul ventures to.

Here is a tip that I can give you regarding how far you need to get in the woods to be farther than everyone else. If there is a trailhead or a gated road, etc., put a camera up to monitor. Clearly it should be a remote location because, remember, we want not many people around. We don't want to do it and pay attention to hunters beyond noticing how many are there. Hunters, you see, aren't moving at a steady pace but, of course, are hunting. We should watch hikers or walkers. Allow an average thirty minutes a mile and check the time they come back by the camera, and you will know how far you need to go to get deeper in the woods than everyone else. This does not mean that Bigfoot is not sometimes in the close-up areas where the parking, tables, road, etc. are, but I think it's clear that the majority of the time during the day, they are in deeper areas, or there would be even more encounters.

I'm not convinced that Bigfoot lives in caves or overhangs long term but rather may weather a storm or stay for a short time. In the mountains of West Virginia there are literally hundreds of miles of caves that haven't been discovered. In addition, there are many vacated and abandoned coal mines where something could seek cover.

A few years ago, I was out hiking in the winter, following coyote tracks in the snow to see where they were spending their time. I came to a rock overhang that had an opening about two feet tall. Shining my flashlight inside, I saw railroad tracks and three small cars on them. I suspect that when mines played out, dirt and debris were shoveled over the entrances, only to settle and expose the openings decades later.

Rights-of-way provide an "edge" for wildlife attraction, and long straight paths that many times avoid human habitation

RIGHTS-OF-WAY

You've seen these from the interstate wherever you live. They are pathways cut through the forests for phone, power lines, or gas lines. They are long; they are straight. Many times, they stay away from most homes. They create edges that deer like to frequent. They enable you to see danger and prey for long distances. West Virginia has rights-of way everywhere because of our energy production.

When looking at an area, I always look for rights-of-way. If I can find an area of wilderness where two of these come together, it might be worth the walk to look around for sign. Once when I was a pretty good ways back in the woods, I came upon one where five came together. I remember thinking with a smile, "This might be a great area for a camera or a perch." Follow the right-of-way on a map and look for places where they cross streams or deep isolated valleys. These can be good starting points for finding active Bigfoot areas.

TOPOGRAPHICAL FEATURES

These might be located on Google Earth, an app, or a topographical map. For people not familiar with topographical maps, they are a type of map that shows the Earth's features using contour lines to show elevation: the closer the lines, the steeper the terrain. A steep mountainside would have lines almost on top of each other, whereas a flat area would have lines relatively far from each other. I like to look for cliffs or rock outcroppings on a high, south-facing hill, in an area that is fairly inaccessible. Look for trails that run along waterways. It would be better if there is a rise or hillside above it. Bigfoot largely enjoy staying above humans and prey. Steep hills or mountainsides are not frequented by most people, so therefore good places for Bigfoot.

Old vacant homesteads produce a lot of Bigfoot activity. Isolated ponds or beaver dams are very attractive to all types of wildlife, as are the parks or preserves that have a lot of acreage and features that are mentioned above but do not allow hunting or have limited entrance. Many roads, ridges, and hollows were named by pioneers and deserve special attention. Any name that includes the words "devil," "ghost," "Indian," or something similar may suggest Bigfoot activity in the past based on cultural stories. One time I hiked for miles in the East Coast's largest wilderness area to camp at "hell for certain branch" just because of this. Just recently in a national park I found a Goblin Knob overlooking Ugly Creek. It would have been a good place to look around if it hasn't changed a lot over the years; remember the halibut effect.

IT'S ALL ABOUT RELATIONSHIPS

The positive thing about putting something out in front of people is that you establish relationships. I get phone calls and messages weekly from people whom I have met or talked to in the past. You never know when this may lead to something "hot," so to speak. It's good to hear old stories from people just to be familiar with them, but for historical purposes, the BFRO database already gives you a good starting place. If you have a full-time job like me, while I find all the reports interesting, there simply isn't enough time to do everything. I must weigh the worth of constantly listening or combing through old reports versus trying to find and listen to Bigfoot activity that has happened most recently.

In the end these are just helpful hints, methods most likely to produce sign or evidence of Bigfoot. I've offered some ways to go to an area you are not familiar with and be able to quickly assess it from a Bigfoot perspective. I can assure you that reports are being investigated all the time in locations that would shock you. Bigfoot go where they want, and in many cases they end up in the most unusual places. It's not uncommon to get a report from a park near a large city, a dump, or near an interstate. You would be surprised how close they live to humans sometimes. The internet, books, and podcasts are littered with such reports. Remember that you only control your land in the daytime, and anything and everything, including Bigfoot, may be creeping around at night.

Well, I talked about how to see signs of Bigfoot presence in a specific area and what to look for. I also suggested looking at the reports in the BFRO database to get an idea of what counties are the most active. Now I want to give you more specific locations based on other factors.

LET'S GET SPECIFIC ON LOCATION

Although there are reports at high elevations in winter, I would suggest staying at lower elevations in cold weather. Weather can change rapidly at high elevations, and animals have a sense of this long before weathercasters do. I remember being with investigators Monongahela and Darren Pevarnik near Spruce Knob (the highest place in West Virginia) in late March. We were in a beautiful area that was very active based on long-duration recorders. We arrived to cool but nice weather only to have a winter storm warning forecasting eight inches of snowfall the following day. Obviously, we bailed out; in retrospect, after we dropped several thousand feet in just a few miles, the weather was great, and I'm sure the Bigfoot had moved as well.

Abandoned homesteads, sheds, and barns are scattered throughout Appalachia and a good place to weather storms and find small animals to feed on

Once again, there should always be water near where you look. If it's a warm and dry year in the high mountains where many of the reports are, then head for sources of water. I like that Summit Lake, in Cranberry Wilderness Area, keeps water year-round even if it's a droughty year. Many state parks in the mountains have ponds or lakes that keep water, like Blackwater State Park. In the western part of the state, there is Beech Fork State Park. Sure, there are lots of rivers and creeks in the higher mountains, but they are long and inaccessible in many places. Remember, we are all about trying to find a Bigfoot, right? Easier to do that by looking around a single body of water.

Make sure to choose areas that you can at least access part of. Sure, the remote locations are great, and I'm all for a couple of day hikes into remote locations that you may like the looks of. In fact, I think that may be the best way to encounter a Bigfoot. It may be curious enough to interact due to fewer human interactions. The halibut effect doesn't apply to remote locations. That being said, remember that they are rare, and in huge areas like the 900,000 acre Monongahela National Forest, they aren't everywhere. For example, many reports come out of Raleigh County. When one looks at maps of the general area around Pipestem State Park and Bluestone Lake, the area looks great. I have spent a couple of dozen overnights in that area over the years, and aside from finding a perch, I encountered no signs or activity. I know Bigfoot are in the area and are seen often, but many places are not that accessible.

I like the Greenbrier River Trail, which runs for many miles and can be easily accessed to locate the remote parts of it. You can look at your maps to determine a remote location or valley that comes up to the trail, and set up camp in that location. Historically, there are a lot of reports from the general region in the BFRO database to help you hone in closer.

If you live close to Charleston like much of the population, there have been sightings in Kanawha State Forest. I spend a lot of time in the woods there, and there are some remote areas you can access from in and around the park. Great mountain biking trails, many of which are closed roadbeds, are safe, easy to travel, and can get you far back in quickly.

If you live in the southern part of the state, Chief Logan State Park is a good location, and in particular, the Wilderness Trail or Devil's Backbone look good. Panther Creek State Park in McDowell County is an area that, while hard to get to, continues to have activity to this day. These are wonderful parks that are underutilized but full of promise. Take a map, pick out a couple of good areas in and around the parks based on the suggestions given earlier. Both parks have a number of features I have talked about, and I wouldn't be surprised at all if you find sign that leads you to believe that it's possible that a Bigfoot could be in the area. As I write this in October of 2022, there was a compelling thermal video shot from behind the lodge last weekend that could be a Bigfoot. Also, don't forget to look for perches at these parks!

A suggestion for the more northern part of the state is Cooper's Rock State Park. I like the canyon, which runs for miles, with parts of it being inaccessible. I noticed the browse line on the trees is very high, indicating an overpopulation of deer there, might be easy pickings for a hungry Bigfoot. There have been reports in and around the campground.

Quite frankly, based on reports, the best thing to do may be to cruise I-64 between Beckley and White Sulfur Springs. Don't forget to put your dashcam on your windshield while cruising. So if there are a lot of reports of road crossings in that area, look at your maps. Are there any parks close by? Is there water nearby or a campground to look for a perch area? Don't forget to look for a corridor to a remote area from the perch, as there has to be one to be a perch.

The reality of Bigfoot in West Virginia is that each county can and may have a honey hole. You know your county better than I do. Are there places that the locals think are haunted? Areas that fit the profile I have given you? Really, it's better for you to find your own private place to spend time looking around.

The advent of the internet and the popularity of Bigfoot television shows, not to mention thousands of podcasts (Don't forget mine! *Wide Open Research*) have put out a lot of information and education that didn't used to be readily available. Although some people don't like the Bigfoot television shows and even find them irritating, I fervently believe that at no time in history has Bigfoot been more popular or acceptable to bring up in conversation. Bigfoot is a monster, so to speak, that many people have grown up with. I think it's exciting, and maybe a romantic thought, to believe that there may be something left to discover, something that man does not know about. I still believe there are still mysteries out there to solve.

Over two hundred ghost towns dot the landscape of the New River Gorge and
Bigfoot is known to haunt the area

CHAPTER 11
THE BIGFOOT REPORTS

"The patterns among eyewitnesses are not demographic, they are geographic; they are not reported by certain types of people who venture into certain areas. This simple pattern suggests an external cause." Matt Moneymaker, Founder of the BFRO and television personality

CLOSE ENCOUNTERS OF THE HAIRY KIND

The following reports are from cases I personally investigated and am including with permission from the BFRO. I met each of the witnesses and conducted the interviews, not just in person, but also as brief and long conversations over the phone.

In every case, I believe that the witnesses were credible, intelligent, and down to earth. Every one of these cases I firmly believe to be accurate reports of substantial merit. I want to share them with you.

The witness reports are reprinted here as the witnesses entered them, except where abbreviations are spelled out. Report numbers are assigned by the BFRO when the report is accepted, so they are not sequential. Notice that this group has collected tens of thousands of reports.

DR. RUSSELL JONES

BFRO REPORT #26380
YEAR: 2009
SEASON: Spring
MONTH: May
DATE: 23rd
STATE: West Virginia
COUNTY: Raleigh County
NEAREST TOWN: Shady Spring
NEAREST ROAD: Shady Spring

OBSERVED: My wife and I were riding an ATV about one mile from an abandoned strip mine. We came up over a small hill and approximately 25-30 yards in front of us and to the right of the trail stood a solid black creature, approximately 8-9 feet tall, standing behind a tree that was only 8-10 inches wide. I saw the creature first and my wife didn't notice until I stopped the ATV and was trying to get it into reverse to turn around. She ask me what I was doing. I said to look at what was standing right over there. When she saw the creature, she started screaming Oh my God, no,no,no,no. I finally got the ATV turned around and left the area as fast as the ATV would run. My wife kept looking behind to see if the creature was following us. Thank God it did not, but I still did not slow down until we were about two miles from the sighting area. I have totally lost interest in outdoor activities that I once loved due to this experience.

ALSO NOTICED: I finally got up the nerve to go back to the sighting area on July 21, 2009. I had three other people with me, all heavily armed. We found some very strange things. Trees pushed over, logs lying over the trail, etc.

OTHER WITNESSES: My wife and I looking for areas to dig ginseng later in the year.

OTHER STORIES: Yes, approximately three other incidents on your site in this area in the past couple of years. Also, about five miles from my sighting area a friend had a deer stolen by something that picked it up and walked off with it. Also, a local police officer said he saw a Bigfoot run across the road in front of him 2-3 miles from my sighting area.

TIME AND CONDITION: Approximately 4:30 PM, sunny skies, approximately 65 degrees.

ENVIRONMENT: Sighting took place on a mountain ridge ATV trail. Lots of poplar, hickory, and oak.

FOLLOW-UP INVESTIGATION: I (Russ Jones) talked to the witnesses (a husband and wife) for about an hour. He is a law enforcement officer, and she is a health care professional at a local hospital.

In addition to what he reported, the following should be added. The husband initially saw the creature about fifty yards away and thought it was a fire-burned stump that he was driving his four-wheeler towards. At about thirty yards he realized he was looking at a huge creature, and he saw it turn its head toward him. The husband was utterly terrified and shocked at the sheer size of the creature.

When describing the creature physically, the husband described the head shape as being similar to that of the 1967 Patterson-Gimlin film subject. The body was much wider across the shoulders than the waist. The creature had very shiny black hair that appeared well groomed. There was some sparse hair on the creature's face. Its forehead sloped back from its very dark eyes. The skin on the face was dark. He described it as "sinister and scary looking." He did not notice any associated odor. The female witness noted how "very erect" the posture of the animal was and noticed how the animal tried to hide behind a smaller tree.

The location is about one mile from the nearest road and about a half mile from an old strip mine site. The sighting took place on a small trail that spurs off from a gas line right-of-way. The location is also on a ridge. There are several small waterways, as well as a three-to-four-acre pond.

BEHIND THE STORY: This is one of the first witnesses I ever interviewed. When we first started talking, he asked me if I had ever seen a Bigfoot. I told him no, and he said, "You just can't believe the size!" He told me it was the size of a "sheet of plywood"! He said, "that a lot of people disappear each year, and I'm not saying they (Bigfoot) have anything to do with it, but they are capable anytime that they want!" He said he was "wearing his pistol and never considered pulling it; the animal was too large."

We talked before about my belief that Bigfoot may use rights-of-way for travel corridors. I further believe that during the day they travel alongside the rights-of-way to stay out of view if they are moving during the day. This witness was travelling on the right-of-way and then took a cut off of it where he ran into the Bigfoot. I believe that in all likelihood, the Bigfoot expected him to continue to travel on the right-of-way.

I took investigator Darren Pevarnik with me to interview the witness and go back to the general area. The witness brought another police officer with him, and they were both holding their weapons and wouldn't put them away. The witness was very emotional and chain-smoked the whole time we were with him. Not only is this witness trained to be a good observer, but he was also clearly traumatized by the encounter.

The wife suffered some post-traumatic stress after the incident. Her husband told me that when they would hear a noise in their neighbor-hood, she would be fearful that Bigfoot was close to their house. I hear from witnesses very often that they think of their sighting almost every day. This general location is one that I have been to many times with multiple different witnesses and have not been able to hone in on a specific area to find the resident Bigfoot population. By any measure, this is an exceptional witness. Skeptics will often talk about how witnesses are often notoriously wrong, and many are, but all it takes is for one out of the tens of thousands of witnesses to be correct and we officially have a new primate.

Related to the weapon comment, this was not the first time I have had witnesses carry or request I carry a weapon when going back to the location of the sighting. I once took a report from a photographer who had been shooting senior photos at a remote pond when some-thing began throwing rocks in the water. It eventually became so aggressive that it scared the student, his father, and the photographer. Investigator Brad Kennan and I took the witness back to the location, but he wouldn't go without us being armed because he was so afraid.

When I originally wrote this years ago, I never carried in the woods unless I was hunting. Now I carry all the time, primarily because of men. I always tell people to carry with you what you need to be comfortable if you have to spend the night in the woods.

BFRO REPORT #31404
YEAR: 2009
SEASON: Fall
MONTH: November
DATE: 11/28/09
STATE: West Virginia
COUNTY: Kanawha
LOCATION DETAILS: 8 miles up Slaughters creek
NEAREST TOWN: Cabin Creek

OBSERVED: In 2009 during rifle buck season (deer) I was hunting in slaughters creek, Kanawha County, West Virginia, out on a logging/mining road when I saw what I thought was a bear until I got about 80 yards from the creature. It was upright, around 7 ½ feet tall and looked like a linebacker, huge. There was a stench in the air like wet dog and body odor as I walked up the road. I must have stepped on a twig or it caught my scent because it turned sharply, made a grunt noise, then in about three steps was up a hillside that it would have taken myself 20-25 steps to go up. It went over the ridge and disappeared into the woods. My eyes were watering from fear, my body was shaking, I had a 30-06 rifle on me, yet I didn't feel like I could have taken a shot. I think I scared it as much as it scared me.

TIME AND CONDITIONS: It was early in the morning on a clear, crisp fall day and the sun had just topped the mountains.

ENVIRONMENT: Wooded area near clear cuts for power lines and close to Remington Coal Mine.

FOLLOW-UP INVESTIGATION: I talked to this witness about his encounter. He is bright, well spoken, and makes a living as an electrician. He was hunting along an old logging road. It was overgrown with trees. He heard a noise that he assumed was a deer coming, and he raised his gun to wait for it. He saw an arm in his scope as the animal raised itself up on the road that he was standing on.

The witness and animal made eye contact without the animal slowing down at all. The witness noted that the nose was humanlike but "flatter." Dark skin around the eyes and nose similar in color to a dog's nose. He also noted wrinkles around the eyes. The hair color was reddish-brown.

BEHIND THE STORY: It's very common for hunters to have sightings. In fact, other than road sightings, hunter sightings are the most common. I have personally interviewed three of these in West Virginia and will go over a fourth shortly. Both of the witnesses I have interviewed were exceptional and bright. This one an electrician and the other had several degrees from West Virginia University.

Ironically, this sighting is just a short distance from downtown Charleston. I have another exceptional report that is just five minutes from downtown Charleston as well, where the witness is a former city councilman and police commissioner. It is amazing the immediate remote wilderness surrounding the capital city. There are rugged mountainsides with little or no housing except around the interstates. Much of the terrain is inhospitable and has no trails.

This witness was on an old logging road that was overgrown. There are four-wheeler paths all over West Virginia. People follow these paths and very seldom get off of them. Newly created logging roads become impassable in a couple of years with nonuse. Many of the mountainsides are just too steep to be ridden on and thus create massive areas that do not see foot or ATV traffic. It is illegal to have ATVs in the nearly million-acre Monongahela National Forest. I have been to this location a few times and couldn't find any reason that this place was any better than the wild wilderness everywhere else around it. For all I know, the world's largest cave or berry patch may be near it and no one knows. The mystery continues.

BFRO REPORT # 28702
YEAR: 2011
SEASON: Winter
Month: January
Date: 5th
STATE: West Virginia
COUNTY: Greenbrier

LOCATION DETAILS: Occurred approximately at 168 mile marker on a long steep hill. Woods on both sides of the highway. No parked vehicles on either side of the road.
NEAREST TOWN: Lewisburg, West Virginia
NEAREST ROAD: I-64

OBSERVED: While driving from Richmond, Virginia, to Charleston, West Virginia, on I-64 I saw what I assumed was a deer run into heavy east bound traffic. One vehicle had to brake hard to avoid hitting this thing. When it came out between cars and hit the grassy 70-foot median it was running like a sprinter runs. I thought, "That's not a deer, that's a man!" He never slowed down when he got into the west-bound lanes and ran right behind a car passing an empty logging truck. He almost ran into the end of the logging truck as he was crossing the road and had to stop. At this time, I saw that he was covered from the top of his head to the ground with long dark brown hair. As soon as the truck passed, he sprinted across the lane and into the woods. The middle of his shoulder was even with the bottom cradle on the log trailer. When I passed this point my 30-year-old son saw him running up the hill through the woods.

OTHER WITNESSES: My son

TIME and CONDITIONS: At 5:05 PM. Sun had just set. It was clear and cold.

ENVIRONMENT: Hardwood Forest on both sides. Appalachian Mountain range.

FOLLOW-UP INVESTIGATION: I talked to the father the same day we received the report. I initially hoped to drive to the spot on I-64, but that day we had a severe winter storm that blanketed all of West Virginia in large amounts of snow. The witness is a retired gentleman, and his son, who also witnessed the Bigfoot, is thirty years old. The witness and I talked on the phone for about forty-five minutes about his sighting, and I found him to be kind, amiable, and believable.

In addition to what the witness initially added, I can add the following: The area where the sighting took place has no nearby houses. There were no vehicles parked on either side of the road. There are woods on both sides of the interstate at this point.

The sighting took place at 5:05 p.m. It was just starting to get dusk. As the animal crossed past the median, the witness noticed that the arms were long and that its posture was bent forward, and its shoulders were hunched forward.

When they initially saw the animal, they were about two hundred yards away, coming towards it. They were very close when the animal was forced to stop for the truck, and the witness noted the hair color and length to be similar to an auburn-colored golden retriever. They were close enough to see the hair "set down" when the creature stopped. Being able to compare the height of the animal to the logging truck, the father believed the animal to be six feet to six feet, six inches tall.

I also talked to the thirty-year-old son, who was in the passenger seat. He told me that he had heard of Bigfoot before but did not know that they were in West Virginia. At the closest point he was about fifty feet from the animal as he was looking out the passenger window as the animal climbed the hill after crossing the interstate. He stated, "I know what I saw, and it was not a person."

I have been in this area many times and have taken another report within five miles of this location about a year earlier. I was on a private expedition with a group of BFRO investigators very close to this location the year before. It is within five miles or so of the Monongahela National Forest. The area of the sighting is significantly lower in elevation than the surrounding mountains, which may mean less severe winter weather. There is also a lot of farm silage in the area, which could be a winter food source. I have found no obvious reason why the Bigfoot chose this spot to cross the interstate. We receive numerous reports of Bigfoot crossing the roads under all types of conditions. Greenbrier County is an area rich in beautiful countryside, remote wilderness, and an abundance of farms and caves.

BEHIND THE STORY: Since that time, I have been to the location above, as well as met the witness, who happens to be a veteran, in person. When I first talked to the witness, he was in Kentucky but had previously run a business in Charleston very close to mine. I was able to track down a few people who were mutual acquaintances who vouched for the credibility and character of the witness.

This Bigfoot road crossing occurred where there have been five others reported within six miles. It's definitely a Bigfoot of unknown origin in terms of why it was there at that location. It's just a few miles from the world-famous Greenbrier Resort, so maybe it was after high-quality leftovers. This is another witness who thinks about his sighting each day. He drove several hours to tell his story to the *Finding Bigfoot* cast when they were in the area. The witness is adamant about what he saw and doesn't care what others believe.

OTHER FAVORITE BFRO REPORTS

These are some of the best reports that I have come across, that although I didn't investigate them myself, I have spoken extensively with the investigator who did. Sometimes I spoke to the witness or other parties involved. Because I know those investigators and respect their intelligence and integrity, I am vouching for these reports as well.

YEAR:2008
SEASON: Winter
MONTH: December
DATE: 26th
STATE: WV
COUNTY: Tucker
LOCATION DETAILS: I do not know the name of the road that leads to this area of the refuge, though it's easy to find. Simply turn left of US Route 32 in front of the small shopping center as you exit Davis, West Virginia. After turning left continue on straight path until you cross a small wooden bridge. After crossing the bridge stay straight on this road and it will lead you to the Camp 70 parking area.
NEAREST TOWN: Davis
NEAREST ROAD: US HIGHWAY 32

OBSERVED: I was hunting West Virginia's late antlerless deer season in the Canaan Valley Wildlife Refuge when the sighting occurred. I had gotten to the area shortly after 3:00 PM that evening, and after parking in the Camp 70 parking area, I hiked up what appeared to be an old logging road trail directly behind the parking area. I had already gotten a late start and wanted to get afield as quickly as possible, so I decided to stalk the logging trail until I got further into the river bottom.

After hunting the trail for about 30 minutes I could see a long distance into the river bottom on my right, so I decided to move into the bottom in hopes a deer would emerge from the thick along the river at dusk. I came across another "road" after leaving the logging trail, so I started walking further into the valley on it. The road was frozen and crusted over due to the cold temperatures, which made traveling quite impossible, so after a short distance I found a small group of trees a few yards from the trail and set up in them.

Shortly after arriving I hear what sounded like brush breaking 150-200 yards below me, towards the river. I readied myself in hopes it was a group of deer moving into the flats to feed, but nothing appeared. A few minutes past and I heard the sound again, and again nothing materialized. I decided to move closer and positioned myself in another group of small trees 100 yards or so below the first site. I had been in this group of saplings 5-10 minutes when I caught movement 80-90 yards below me and to the left. I could see the movement with my naked eye, and immediately upon seeing it I scoped the group of trees and to my surprise saw nothing.

A few minutes went by, and I caught movement again, I quickly scoped the trees, and this time I was shocked by what I saw. At first, I thought it was a large man, as the first thing I saw in my scope was a vague silhouette, but when my eyes focused, I could see what appeared to be a primate-like creature standing upright and staring directly at me. It only broke its stillness to slightly move the upper portion of its body in an up and down motion. It would bend its knees as if to sit down, then immediately stand back up.

This went on for what seemed to be over a minute, then the creature exited the group of trees and moved to my left (the creature's right), towards the mountain behind me. It walked across an expanse of river basin that I would guess to be 70-80 yards long before entering the timber and exiting my field of view. It kept watching me the whole time it was walking, only breaking it's stare a few times to look directly in front of it.

I initially thought of trying to locate its tracks, but my nerves got the best of me, and I started moving to the parking lot as quickly as I could. Though the creature never made any threatening movements, I didn't feel safe enough to continue hunting and remain in the valley any longer after the sun had went down if I had to. I immediately left the area and had no further incidents on my way to the vehicle.

ALSO NOTICED: Nothing else unusual was seen nor heard.

OTHER WITNESSES: No other witnesses.

TIME AND CONDITIONS: Evening. The sun was just starting to go down, though there was still sufficient light for clear vision.

ENVIRONMENT: The area was a large river basin surrounded by mountains. The river is shrouded in pine and rhododendron thickets.

FOLLOW-UP INVESTIGATION BY INVESTIGATOR CATHY BETZ: I spoke to Mr. X over the phone, and he described his encounter in greater detail.

After watching the figure of what initially looked like a large man, Mr. X determined it was not a man at all, but an upright, bipedal creature that was covered in hair. The creature was looking back at him the whole time, even when it walked to its right before eventually entering the thicker timber. Mr. X was about 80-90 yards away and saw the creature through the clearing with both with the aid of his rifle scope and with his naked eye. He was able to give a very detailed description of the creature, which he viewed for several minutes.

It looked to be approximately six feet tall and around 250 lbs. He could not make a clear determination of its gender.

It was covered with six-to eight-inch-long hair that was shaggy in some places and flowing in others, particularly in the arms, where he could see the hair flowing with the movements. He describes the color as black, with white-gray, or "salt and pepper" highlights, much like an adult gorilla's hair.

The face had a prominent nose that was not full, like a human, but not as sparse as a chimp. He states that it was primarily flat. The skin on the face was a uniform light gray color. Mr. X commented that he had seen drawings of Bigfoot and that compared to those, this one had rather sparse facial hair. The lips were slightly parted and the same flesh color as the face. The teeth were easily seen and were described as being much like a German Shepherd's teeth; straight front teeth with prominent canines approximately 3/4 of an inch long. The ears were not clearly visible. Mr. X stated that the ears were either somewhat pointed, or that it had pointed tufts of hair around the ears. It had a brow ridge that was less prominent than an ape, but more than a human. The eyes were very big and coal black with no white visible sclera.

The head of the creature was slightly conical, less than a gorilla, but more than a human. The shoulder width was in proportion to the size of a human with the same body mass. Mr. X did not notion any details about the hands as he was focused on the face.

The gait of the creature was very fluid and more elongated than a human would walk. Its movements were unhurried and precise.

There was no odor associated with the encounter.

The creature didn't make any noises, nor did it make any threatening gestures. Mr. X stated that he did not feel intimidated by the creature's presence, but that he did feel nervous about staying in the area. He stated "the fading light and the feeling of unease were the main reasons that I didn't attempt to pursue any evidence of my encounter. There was still ample light to see a great distance over the river basin."

Mr. X stated that he has hunted all of his life and has never seen anything resembling what he recently witnessed. He had heard of Bigfoot before but did not pay it much mind until he actually saw one. I found Mr. X to be sincere, honest, and forthright. And, from Mr. X's physical and behavioral description of the creature, it is in my opinion that what he saw was a very young, or juvenile Bigfoot.

As a side note, when I asked Mr. X if he had ever noticed anything unusual about the area, such as stick structures, he recalled a remarkable observation. He told me that he had noticed rocks that were stacked on top of each other. He had thought that they were being left by hikers, or hunters, but found it odd that they were found not near any trails or paths. He stated that they were composed of flat rocks that were anywhere from two to six rocks high. This, of course, could have been made by humans, but is also a known behavioral characteristic that is associated with Bigfoot habitation.

BEHIND THE STORY: Cathy Betz is an experienced outdoors person. She is a nurse and an amateur naturalist. She is also perceptive and very bright. She was also very impressed with this story and believed it to be true.

Canaan Valley Wildlife Refuge is an interesting area surrounded by the Dolly Sods Wilderness Area, the Monongahela National Forest, Canaan Valley State Park, Blackwater State Park, and some private property. The refuge itself is about seventeen thousand acres, sits in a basin, and is surrounded by mountains. The Blackwater River flows sleepily through it. It is one of the highest wetlands in the eastern United States. It has a few walking trails, but not many, and it's not visited by many people. When you are there in warm weather, the grasses are head high in many places, and you can't see very far.

Several years ago, because of this report and several others in the area, investigator Darren Pevarnik and I were spending a lot of time in this area. We would meet every few months for a few days to spend time in and near the refuge with witnesses, or just to hike around. We have heard wood knocks, rock clacks, and vocals there. This is also the location where we found beechnuts cracked open on a large rock. This is also the location where I got "spooked" one time in the middle of the night!

Once, Darren and I went midweek, and there was no one around anywhere. We drove back into a remote area and hiked a couple of miles farther into the basin. It was a very foggy night, which is common there. In the gloom, something approached, very close, and whistled at us. I looked around through the Flir thermal imager, but the night fog was thick and getting foggier. By the time we left, we had to walk out using the thermal because in places we couldn't even see in front of us at all.

Speaking of spooked, one time during an expedition, investigator Brad Kennan was leading a group into wilderness in the dark. Once they got set up and had no lights on, they heard movement. Brad saw a flying squirrel, which are active at night, on thermal and told the group. A little while later the squirrel made another sound; then there were large sounds and crashing inside his group. Brad flipped on his headlight to find the large, muscular man in his group facing the woods, legs flexed, eyes huge, preparing to be attacked!

Funny as it is, the woods are completely different at night. Familiar places seem unfamiliar, and in the deep woods it's easy to get turned around. For safety's sake, I have gone to using satellite-based apps on my cell phone so I don't need cell service. West Virginia is in the process of having cell service in most parks, but it's sketchy, and there is no cell service in the wilderness.

The *Finding Bigfoot* television show has been to the area, and the expeditions experienced significant Bigfoot activity. It's a wonderful place to visit any time of the year with world-class skiing in the winter and all forms of activity in the warm months. Plus, if you want to escape the heat of summer, with high elevations, much of West Virginia is comfortable and can be ten degrees cooler than everywhere else.

I mentioned previously that this is one of the reports that made many of us think that Bigfoot do not worry about colder weather as much as we do, as this is a cold-weather report at high elevation. The mountains surrounding this area drop off steeply, and lower elevations are easily accessible if it's desired. I would give anything to know what that Bigfoot was doing down by the river for the time that the hunter was there. These little pieces of behavior would help us know so much in predicting where to find these animals if we could answer them.

BFRO REPORT #12959
YEAR: 1989
SEASON: Winter
MONTH: November
DATE: 23
STATE: West Virginia
COUNTY: Randolph
DIRECTIONS TO LOCATION: Southern Randolph County
NEAREST TOWN: Elkwater

OBSERVED: It happened in 1989 on a hunting trip to the middle region of West Virginia. We were on our yearly deer hunting trip in the remote mountainous area of Randolph County. I was about 24 years old and in on leave from the military on the family hunting trip. My family and friends have hunted this area for many years, and I was very comfortable and familiar with the area.

The road back had not been traveled for years and was very washed out with and overgrown with brush. It was about 7-8 miles before we came to impassable areas of the road, and it was then that we geared up and proceeded on foot. I would estimate we had gone another 2-3 miles on foot before we reached the crest of the mountain and decided to find our hunting spots.

The light had just begun to peak over the mountaintop when I cleared my spot and settled in. I had worked up a pretty good sweat on the steady pace up the mountain, so it was not long after setting and listening to the first morning light and waking up the rest of the forest I began to nod off to sleep. After going in and out a few times I decided to get up and move around a little to try to wake myself up.

After about 20 minutes of walking around I stumbled onto a very old wooden tree stand. Although I could tell that it had been there many years, I remember thinking it was in the best spot the very visible and open woods just under the crest of the hilltop. Not too long after that, I ate the apples and oranges I had brought. After a while the warm morning sun took its toll on me, and I nodded off again.

A bad smell woke me right up. The forest was completely quiet around me and all I could think of was what the hell that awful smell was. As I became more alert, I could hear rustling below me and what I thought were some faint grunts and whines. I decided it was time to lean over and get a visual on it.

It was about 25 feet below me on the slope and directly in front of the stand. It was not aware of my presence above it. It was about 5 feet tall with long dark, reddish-brown hair. The hair from its head down was equal length, about 2-3 inches long. The hair went down its arms and hands as well as its feet. I could barely see fingernails and toe nails, not claws but nails like a human.

Most of its hair was tangled and matted in spots as if it had wallowed the ground or a tree or something. I watched it smelling the orange peels and apple core then tasting them. It looked around at one point as if to wonder where they came from. I wondered how long it would be before it became aware of my presence and what it would do when it did.

Then I heard rustling coming down from the top of the hill, loud rustling, and I could tell that something was coming at a pretty rapid speed. I saw the one below me turn and look in the direction of the noise. It froze for a few seconds and looked almost like a statue.

I could not see at this point what was coming down the hill. I was leaning to my right and looking down. I tried to move my eyes to the left, but my view was blocked by the trees that was holding my stand and partially by the full brim hat that I was wearing. I kept moving my eyes between the one below me and the direction of the disturbance coming down the hill.

As it moved toward our position it began to make noises like I have never heard before. I would ordinarily not be able to describe the noise, but I have read where other people have described it as a record being played backward. I would have to say that is a very close description. It is as if it were speaking a language but like nothing that I had ever heard before.

The one below me sprang to its feet and then moved 15-20 feet to the right of me. It moved very rapidly, kind of between a run and a leap, all on its feet though. It did not use its arms. It then started to bellow back at the one coming down the hill and it sounded almost like they were arguing. That is the impression that it left with me anyways.

It wasn't until the one behind me came into clear view that I started to feel very scared. As it came into my immediate area it moved toward the first one and began to slow to what became very cautious movements. Its attention seemed to move between the first creature and its surrounding area. I felt at this moment it was alert to my presence.

This second one was much larger than the first one and it seemed very irritated. The bigger one was covered with very dark hair, almost black. It was very muscular, and its arms were noticeably long. It stood with a slight bend but an upright posture. It had to be 8-9 feet tall. It was much larger than a human.

As these two creatures squabbled (communicated?) back and forth, their gestures were extremely humanlike. I was under the impression that the larger one was scolding the smaller one.

They moved about 40-50 feet to the right of me. At this point the larger one had its back to me; I could make out facial features on the smaller one. It had very human-like features but a different nose. Hair covered most of the face, but it looked to be thin hair, not like the rest of it.

Then the smaller creature spotted me because it crouched and then went into a squatting position and looked in my direction. Their chattering began to quiet and then the larger one, with its back still to me, went into a squatting position for a few seconds. The smaller one then began to howl and bellow very loudly. The larger one with its back to me began to howl very loudly also. The larger creature then pushed the smaller one and the smaller one sprang to its feet and rapidly ran across the hill on my right. It ran in long leaping strides and moved very fast like nothing I had ever seen. I never noticed it ever look back.

As the smaller one ran, the larger one stood up and slowly turned toward me. It had one arm bent above its forehead as if it were shading or hiding its eyes. It stood very straight and tall and looked directly at my tree stand.

All of the fear from before overcame me again, and I prayed this thing did not try to come up my tree. I thought for an instant that I would yell at it, jerk or jump and maybe frighten it away but I could not even bring myself to move. I could not even bat an eye. I could feel my legs starting to shake and I became hot all over. For an instant I thought that I was going to pass out or become physically ill.

For a brief moment it looked right at my face. From what I could see it had very humanlike eyes and very large round nostrils. I could not make out the lips because of the hair on the face but I would guess that they were think lips because the hair didn't stick out. It did not have much of a protruding mouth or jaw like an ape. It had a fairly flat face like a human.

It put its arm to its side and began to look around. It swiveled at the hips and looked in every direction. After a quick glance back at me it began to walk off in the direction the smaller one had gone. It did not run, or act scared at all. It made very long howls as it walked and turned back a few times to look in my direction as it walked away.

I watched it and listened until it just became a black figure moving through the woods. I could hear it howl or bellow a few more minutes. Then I heard what sounded like something beating a tree or log with a tree or log with a limb or stick or something.

After about thirty minutes I decided that if it meant to do me harm, it sure had its chance, and it was probably safe to get down out of the tree stand. I made my way back toward my friend that I had left earlier that morning. I never even thought to check the ground for evidence or anything.

After about an hour I walked up on my friend and could see his blaze orange through the trees. I very carefully made my way in his direction. As I approached him, I could see that he was staring at me. He was sitting against some downed trees and didn't move a muscle. As I moved closer to him, I smiled and ask if he had seen anything. He was very pale, and I could tell he was a little scared and puzzled and answered to me that he was not sure what he had seen.

I jokingly said, "You look like you saw a Bigfoot!" and he jumped to his feet and asked, "Did you see it?"

I nodded to him, yes, then he began to tell me what he saw. Apparently, the larger creature had moved across the hill in front of him, crashing through the trees about 40-50 yards away. He said at first, he thought it was a bear but after observing it, he could plainly see that it was moving very fast and walking upright like a man.

I said we should try to track the two creatures, but it really didn't take too much for him to talk me out of it.

This really happened, 16 years ago in Randolph County, West Virginia.

ALSO NOTICED: I have never returned to that area of the woods.

OTHER WITNESSES: 2 witnesses, hunting.

TIME AND CONDITIONS: 9:00 AM. Slightly overcast, but clear weather.

ENVIRONMENT: Top of the mountain, open woods: oak, maple, hickory, beech, walnut, and pine.

FOLLOW-UP INVESTIGATION BY BFRO INVESTIGATOR STEPHEN WILLIS: I contacted the witness on November 25, 2005, and I spoke to him about the incident. He is credible and I believe he accurately described what he observed that day.

BEHIND THE STORY: I have known Steve Willis for years. He is retired from the US Army, a business owner, an experienced woodsman, and always calls things the way that he sees them. I have talked to him about this report a couple of times, and he simply says, "They definitely saw what they claim." He never got to talk to the second witness; apparently, he didn't want to talk about it and moved on with his life.

The symptoms the first witness exhibited are consistent with a panic attack. I have a sneaking suspicion that the reason that there aren't even more sightings is the "sixth sense." People are in the outdoors and get a feeling of something watching them, uneasiness, hair on neck standing up, and/or anxiety. Maybe it's not even a conscious decision that they turn around, leave an area, or move in a different direction.

I think that our ancestors, even a few generations ago, were more sensitive to the woods and their surroundings. Quite frankly, their lives depended upon it. I know that even though I am in the woods often, it takes me a while to slow down and start to get in tune with the woods around me. The woods announce our presence to everything as soon as we step in it, with birds, chipmunks, and various other vermin protesting our intrusion into their world.

It's a challenge for many to see something that they don't believe to exist, as it forces us to reevaluate the very foundations on which we have built our lives. I have other sightings by two brothers, both engineers, where one was very descriptive about what they saw and the other just saying he saw something but doesn't know what it was or want to talk about it.

This report too took place in the general area of Kumbrabow State Park. The park is located in Randolph County and doesn't see a lot of visitors compared to other parks in West Virginia.

A couple of points that I found interesting about the report were the apparent communication between the animals. The howling going on after the sighting makes me wonder if they weren't "calling" or trying to communicate with other Bigfoot in the family group. It seems to me as if the juvenile was left in the general area of the mountaintop and the adult was off doing whatever but discovered humans were in the area and went charging back to where the juvenile should be or was left. Apparently, it must have smelled the witness at one point, as it was looking around for him.

On a side note, I went and stayed at the park to attempt to go to the exact location of the sighting, though many years later. At night, this was the darkest place I had ever been in my life, and I literally couldn't see my hand in front of my face.

BFRO REPORT #13949
YEAR: 1970's
SEASON: Spring
MONTH: March
DATE: 30
STATE: West Virginia
COUNTY: Berkeley County
LOCATION DETAILS: Knipetown Road about seven miles down route 11 North, approximately 7 miles north of Martinsburg, West Virginia and to the west of Route 11.
NEAREST TOWN: Knipetown
NEAREST ROAD: Knipetown road

OBSERVED: It was back in the early 1970s, springtime, late at night (around 2 AM). I was out driving down a road that had a farm on one side and an apple orchard on the other. As I was driving there was some movement about 200 yards in front of me on the roadway going from the farm to the orchard. When the object got in the middle of the road it turns its head and looked in my direction, at this time I got a really good look at it, about 8-9 feet tall, very heavy build, long lanky arms, long dark red hair, very long stride (about two and a half steps to cross the road). If I was to guess the weight, it would have been 400-500 pounds.

I was on a road with very little traffic (I was the only one on the road at the time). I have to admit that I was not a Bigfoot believer until that night. I didn't tell anyone about this because I knew they would not believe me. I was one of the chief officers in our local fire department at the time and I didn't want people to think I was nuts. Oh, by the way, I did get close enough to see what it was or wasn't. I know I was shaken up a bit and did not travel that road for a long time afterwards.

ALSO NOTICED: I didn't stick around, too shook up at what I just seen.

OTHER STORIES: No, none in the area; that is another reason that I didn't say anything.

CONDITIONS: Large farm on the south side of the road and large apple orchard on the north side of the road.

FOLLOW-UP INVESTIGATION BY BFRO INVESTIGATOR MIKE ARAGONA: I spoke with the witness over the phone on 5/16/2006. The witness, a former chief in his local fire department, was very adamant about what he saw.

Additional facts:

The sighting took place at approximately 2 AM.

The hair on the animal was somewhat uniform length. He estimated it to be six inches long or so. It had reddish-brown color.

When the animal looked in the direction of the witness, the eyes had a glare from the headlights of the vehicle.

His impression was that it was a male.

The witness kept driving because he was surprised at what he saw. This was the only encounter that he ever had.

BEHIND THE STORY: One of the reasons that reports like this appeal to me is that the witness is a respected member of our society. I mentioned earlier that I myself have interviewed policeman, deputies, a mayor, city councilman, firefighters, teachers, scientist, electricians, hunters, veterans, loggers, park rangers, and doctors. Witnesses are a wide and varied cross section of our society and only bonded in many cases by the fact that they live where Bigfoot does; they are geographic and not demographic.

Often people will ask what it was that convinced me the most that Bigfoot is real. I reply, in the end, short of seeing one clearly, it is the witnesses and the things that I have found in the woods. In this case, investigator Darren Pevarnik is familiar with this witness personally and knows him to be believable and of good character. It was at night, which is when most of the road sightings take place. While also solitary, Bigfoot is largely believed to be a nocturnal creature, which is the most probable reason we don't have even more sightings. I think Bigfoot behaves much like a big old buck. You will see them out in the day rarely, for breeding, a special type of feeding, or if they have been jumped or disturbed, but largely they stay in an inaccessible area until after dark.

What was the reason for Bigfoot to be in this area? A special treat? It wasn't the apples because they ripen from June through the fall, so it was too early for that. If I lived in this area, I would be driving around looking at that time of the year, trying to figure it out. Obviously, Bigfoot would love apples and so do deer, a primary food source; you wouldn't be surprised at all that either would be caught in an orchard at night when the apples are ripening. This case also appeals to me because I would be wondering if that particular creature doesn't hang around all through the year since it was there when the apples weren't ripe. Looking at a map, we can see an area of wilderness with water within a few miles of the sighting. It might be a good place to get out and look at.

As you can see, an investigation starts with the witness. If it's a good report, then there are usually a couple of interviews, emails, texts, etc. Next is going to the site to see the area in person. Typically, before I even meet or talk with someone, I have looked at the area of the incident on a topo map and a satellite photo. The most important thing, once the witness is deemed reliable, is always trying to figure out why the animal was there. Can you figure out where it came from or where it may have been going? Have there been other sightings in that area, and if so, at what time of the year?

One of the things that are hard to account for are habituators. You would probably never know that there was a habituator in the area. Once again, habituators are individuals who either knowingly or unknowingly have been feeding, gifting, or providing security to a Bigfoot or group of Bigfoot. Some believe that they do exchange gifts with Bigfoot. For example, leaving a candy bar out somewhere like a stump may get you a feather, special stick, rock, etc. in return. I'm not making a judgment on this but rather just reporting. There have been whole books written about it. Many of us have relationships with people who make these claims.

Maybe these people post their land and don't let anyone on it, providing a sanctuary. Many times these people become protective of the animals and don't want people to bother them even if it's to collect evidence. They may know that they are feeding "something" but are not even sure what it is. It's hard to know where these people are or might be when trying to account for a Bigfoot in an area. I would guess the number of habituators is in the hundreds for sure, but this is largely just a guess based on the number of cases in my general region I am familiar with, or other ones that investigators have shared with me.

I think that some of the best evidence, outside of a body, may come from these habituators in the future, as they have better access to the animals than others. For whatever reason, many times these people are hesitant to try to get real and concrete evidence. Seemingly the experience becomes what is important for them.

There have been literally dozens of known cases at any time going on across the country. The BFRO has been involved in some of these cases and have collected some evidence, much of it not having been released due to future documentaries. The evidence that has been acquired in some of these cases is "owned" by individuals who may or may not want to share it with the public for whatever reason. Some evidence is clear video and compelling. Keep in mind that even if they put it out there for everyone to look at on a website or YouTube, many would refuse to believe it, so it may have to be more than a video.

One last thought. At present we have yet to receive any substantial evidence from someone claiming to be a habituator. After a recent podcast I did on the habituator topic, my eldest niece, who lives on an Ohio farm, said, "If it was bothering them that much, I don't understand why they just didn't shoot it. I would have." It's a good argument that the evidence that is the deciding factor may come from someone who has them messing around with their property and just shoots one.

MORE COMPELLING REPORTS

Again, I present more reports, some mine, some friends', some recent, some historical. These are reports presented for two reasons: First, they are compelling, and second, the witnesses were unusually credible and sensible. I post some clarifying thoughts after each report. As I get reports from all over the country, I decided to include some not in West Virginia, as it's still the same creature with decidedly similar behaviors across North America.

HUNTER HAS SIGHTING

DATE OF ENCOUNTER: 11/14/20 11:00 AM
LOCATION: Core, West Virginia (near Morgantown)

OBSERVED: I had been sitting for around an hour in a tree stand. Little wind, sunny skies. Heard footsteps. Assumed they were close as they were heavy/loud. Sounds came from behind and to the right of me. Wind was right to left. Kept getting louder. This is when I was able to determine it wasn't a four-footed gait. I assumed it was a person although the woods in that direction are thick and no real trails. No houses for miles. As it got closer I could see a dark figure. It stopped roughly parallel to me. 35 yards downhill, brush was shoulder height on me, was mid-torso on the figure. I couldn't reconcile what I was seeing at first. I thought it was a man, but I am 5'8" tall. This was 8-10 inches taller. Not extraordinarily heavy build. It reminded me of a late teenagers body, slim and muscular. Dark brown, almost black. Heavy brow ridge. Wide nose. Chin thrust forward a bit. Head to a slight conical shape. Arms appeared longer than a humans would be. Couldn't see lower body. It stood still. It didn't see me but apparently sensed or heard something. Wind had stopped and was blowing in my face. The creature (I don't know what else to call it) raise its head and appeared to sniff the air. It grunted and turned to the right, went into the brush, and was gone. I could hear it for a few minutes. I realized it was very quiet. Total time was maybe 30-45 seconds.

OTHER POINTS OF INTERVIEW: The witness was a coal miner for

a couple of decades and now works in maintenance. He doesn't hunt a lot anymore; he usually fishes most of the time. He saw the creature from the waist up and noticed an oblong face. The creature wasn't bulky, but instead was leaner. He got the impression that maybe it was younger. He noticed that when it turned its head, it turned from the waist, not really turning its head so much. He didn't notice ears, but the nose was wide and flattened. He has since hunted in the same stand but has not had any other type of encounter either there or elsewhere in his life. I was the first person he told about the encounter. He thought that it was a weird place for the animal to be, as the woods were broken up by fields and not a huge expanse of wilderness. My thanks to Cliff Barackman, of *Finding Bigfoot*, for the referral.

BEHIND THE SCENES: If it's not a person in a car that had a sighting, hunters are most likely to have one. It's not usually when they are moving around but rather when sitting. We hear about the large, flattened nose so much, but it seems that sense of smell is most likely not the greatest sense that they have. It's very common for people to report that the Bigfoot acted as though it had smelled them or attempted to.

BFRO REPORT #74981
YEAR: 2015
SEASON: FALL
MONTH: October
DATE: 10/17/2015
STATE: West Virginia
COUNTY: Wyoming County
NEAREST TOWN: Kopperston
NEAREST ROAD: Rout 99

OBSERVED: I have spent my whole life in the woods in this area. Me and my stepson were ginseng hunting in an area that I had been through multiple times. We decided to try the opposite side of the ridge that we went to the weekend before and harvested a pretty sizable amount of ginseng.

As we drop down from the ridge and began going around the hill we noticed the area that we were in was a little darker, due to excellent shade cover from the large timber in that area. As a result there was a lot of moss, chicken of the woods, and other mushrooms.

As we started to through the swag, off of a small point that we were on, we began to hear some unusual sounds. One of the sounds resembled almost like laughter. What was so strange is that it was low but echoed.

You could see really good under the timber. There's some small trees, but no thick brush so we kind of ignored it and wrote it off as just an unusual sound of a bird. We heard this sound 5 or 6 times.

Just a few seconds after we heard a low growling sound that didn't resemble and kind of bear or coyote that I had heard. I yelled "hey bear you get out of here" in an attempt to possibly scare off any type of predator in the area. I had seen several bears in the area over the years and actually harvested two with my stepson.

The next moment a loud sound that almost resembled an ambulance siren or a siren on a vehicle, but with more depth in the tone, rang out through the woods. Then a few seconds of a sound that was a long huff huff huff that was very guttural and grungy came through the woods.

We stood silent until he said he wants to leave. I'm scared as he was. He was only about 13 at the time. I told him to just hold on and I'm sure it was nothing. I had a Glock 21 SF with me, which is a 45 caliber handgun and was pretty confident we could handle anything in the woods.

Suddenly, about 60 yards away, the tops of the trees started swaying back-and-forth and you could hear the sounds of feet moving quickly in the leaves, but it didn't sound like any bear, deer, or squirrel moving. The steps were heavy, but yet so fast paced. There was a grouping of trees, beech, maple, and hickory, between 8 and 24 inches in diameter. None of the larger trees were shook. The smaller trees 8-16 in diameter were swaying back-and-forth violently, and the tops were banging against each other. I looked around and there was no wind blowing at this time.

The large timber in the area somewhat blocked our view of the creature doing this from where we were standing, but occasionally we would get a glimpse of what appeared to be a large creature on two legs approximately 6-7 feet tall moving from one smaller tree before shaking the tree hard enough that it would bang against the tops of the other trees. This occurred for 3 to 5 minutes.

It is notable that the creature always positioned itself on the backside of the tree, keeping the tree between us. It stopped for about 30 seconds. There was no sound in the woods whatsoever. Then we heard quick footsteps going through the leaves. As we moved to try to catch a glimpse of whatever it was, we could see a large creature brownish black on two legs moving quickly, but as it moved between the trees. It was so fast we could only catch glimpses of the creature. It was putting distance between us.

All of the sudden the trees started shaking again. Trees 6 to 8 inches in diameter were being violently shaken violently. Branches were falling from the tops as they banged together. Then a tree began to crack and within a few seconds it quickly fell. The tree was probably 20 to 25 feet high, give or take, and 6 to 8 inches in diameter. After this tree had fallen, another tree, similar in size, but much taller began to shake violently until it cracked and fell to the ground. 5-6 trees were broken in this manner.

Then as quickly as it started, it all stopped. You could hear the sound of something crossing the point in the distance with heavy, quick steps. We decided to go down into the area. Well I did, he was in shock and near tears, but I had the firearm so he went with me.

There were all sorts of small trees freshly broken in the area. The larger trees we had seen broken were all broken in the same way, pointing downhill. As we investigated the area where the creature had been, we heard what sounded like rocks being rolled down the hill. I looked up on the point in front of us and could see large rocks, the size of a basketball, maybe a little larger, being rolled down the point, not toward us but close enough it would scare us.

I looked up toward the ridge of the point. I could see a creature near a large, old squatted. I thought it was a stump at first, but then it moved quickly to the other side of the tree, blending in with the shade and remaining hunched or squatted.

I stared at what I thought was the creature momentarily. The woods were completely still. I turned to my stepson and told him that we would go exactly the way we came. As I was leaving I remembered I had a pb&j sandwich in my bag. I laid it on a stump as to say I respect this is your home and to say "eat this instead of me."

I have been back through the area and heard strange sounds, but never had any more incidents. Each time I leave a small gift like a pop tart or a candy bar. Close to that area are large stacks of rocks that are uniform and almost rectangular. The stacks are usually level on top and measure 2'h by 6' in length, and 4' wide.

Several areas have dug out holes against old logs that appeared to either wallowed or some kind of bedding area. I do not fear this creature in the least, but I respect it immensely. The property is now leased by a hunting club and I am worried that they will disrupt his home as they do not respect mother nature, but rather feel above it.

ALSO NOTICED: Rocks stacked in neat, organized piles. Rocks were 30-50 pounds lbs. and were obviously placed. A lot of small timber, 3-5 inches, broken against trees in the area.

TIME AND CONDITIONS: Around 4 p.m. under clear skies. The weather was perfect to be in the woods. It was in the low 70s and absolutely beautiful.

ENVIRONMENT: Typical Appalachian Mountain landscape with lots of big, hardwood timber. There are a lot of fallen trees in the area along with moss, mushroom, and elderberry on the ridge. There are a lot of old mines in the area and small hollows with water.

FOLLOW-UP INVESTIGATION REPORT BY BFRO INVESTI-GATOR DR. RUSS JONES: I interviewed the witness at length as well as many other communications. I can add the following:

The witness is an avid and knowledgeable outdoorsman. He spends a lot of time year-round in remote and hard-to-get-to locations. This particular location is a four-hour walk off-trail. Many times, ginseng hunters are forced to go where others won't, in hopes to find a lot of the root. The witness is thirty-three and has a degree in counseling. He grew up and lives in a very remote and mountainous area of West Virginia.

The section of the woods they had walked through had been fire burned years before, but they were dropping into a holler that was dark and had a lot of large timber. When the encounter initially happened, he thought someone was within fifty yards laughing but couldn't see anything at that time. Next, they heard a deep and husky growl. That was when he noticed the trees sixty yards away begin to shake. As it continued to shake the trees and move away from them, it always stayed behind a tree, and even with all the leaves on the ground, it made much less noise than one would expect for something that size.

He had been in the area previously and had heard some unusual sounds but had no idea what they were. He's very familiar with game sounds, having hunted and killed most game, including deer and two bear.

When he went to where the trees had been broken, there were others there that had been broken previously. The trees were broken by pulling them toward the creature and were all lying at a 6:30 to 7:00 direction.

The witness just recently told his wife for the first time. His stepson is afraid to go back in the woods now.

I find the witness believable and compelling. Like so many witnesses, he has now become interested in the subject. Maybe he will be like so many of us and have a lifelong interest after an encounter.

BEHIND THE SCENES: A couple of points on this great report. The pile of rocks. Some believe that Bigfoot may bury their dead, including the possibility of covering them with rocks as some other mammals may do. It's something to keep in mind, but most likely it's rock piles gathered by pioneers when they made fields. If you could see how steep it is in some of these locations, it's shocking the amount of work it would take. Also, with the trees being snapped by pulling and being on the ground at the 6:30 to 7:00 location. Many times, the assumption is that trees are being pushed rather than pulled, and that's what you hear from most people. The position they were lying in may mean a dominance of handedness. The sticks, I assume, came to the dominant side. No one can say for sure, but it's something to keep in mind and consider in the future.

This witness is one of the best ones that I have talked to not only because he is bright, but because of how much time he is in the woods. Commonly, he gets a couple of pounds of ginseng in a day, and that's hard to do nowadays unless you are really in the most remote of places. He's spent a lot of time looking on maps and identifying locations he believes might be a good place for a Bigfoot to be. I have reminded him, me being a huge map nerd myself, that there are many more great Bigfoot locations in the woods than there are Bigfoot.

A SCARY ENCOUNTER FROM EAST TENNESSEE

WITNESS: 18-year-old female (50 now)
LOCATION: Cherokee National Forest (east Tennessee)
DATE: End of August 1992

OBSERVED: The witness moved to Tennessee from south Florida, and while a city girl, she quickly grew fond of the country life in east Tennessee. She grew to enjoy horseback riding, a newfound hobby, and camping with her family. One of the places they went camping commonly was the Laurel Falls are of the Cherokee National Forest, which was 30 miles or so away. The witness enjoyed the location so much and was so comfortable there that after her senior year in high school, right before college, a group of friends decided to go there for a week of camping.

Her best friend and her went two days earlier than everyone else to enjoy themselves. Once in the remote area of the park they parked at a wide spot and hiked the 20 minutes to a post card pretty setting by a stream where she had camped many times with her family.

The girls had a carload of camping gear and began trips back and forth. The first trip when they got to the campsite they heard something that sounded like two 2x4's banging together. They yelled hello but didn't hear anything. As they made several trips carrying their gear they both continued to hear the "bangs" when approaching camp. By the middle of the afternoon all the gear was carried in and they didn't hear anything else. They had a nice meal and an uneventful evening.

The next day they decided to do the two hour hike to the falls. They had a nice walk there, laughing and telling stories, and ate lunch. They had walked about an hour and a half back when one of the girls lost the pin in her watch and it fell off.

Admittedly, the 20 minutes they looked for the pin was the first time they had been quiet the whole trip. Off to the left and through the thick rhododendron bushes, near a creek, they heard a noise like someone may have been making fun of them, na-na-na-na, they heard it again and decided it was their friends coming the next day had come early and were trying to scare them. They wanted to see so they snuck the 7-8 steps through the bushes on a deer trail. They could see the creek through the bushes another 7-8 steps away narrowly through the brush. They could hear noise and something in the creek but because of the narrow opening they couldn't see what it was. They crept up and stepped out expecting to see their friends and heard another noise that sounded like a record player being played backwards.

In an instant, they went from laughing to horrified. When they had stepped completely through the bushes motion went everywhere, but standing in the creek to the left 15' away was this "thing." She couldn't breathe. She couldn't believe that it was real. It was crouched, not all the way down or up, and holding perfectly still, She was terrified.

Just then to the right, just out of sight was these rapid "clacking" sounds. She looked right in that direction but didn't see anything and when she looked back the creature was leaning way backwards, almost like it was falling, but holding still. She put her fists up in horror, and when she scooted her feet the creature popped straight back up unbelievably fast.

From the area of the clacking sound came a growl. A low deep growl, it was unnatural. Looking that way, she still couldn't see anything. She looked back at the creature, and it was slowly backing up. The creature took the back of its hand and flung it at them while saying "WAH" very loudly.

As the creature walked slowly, almost unnaturally, smooth backwards, it crossed its feet with each step while slight crouched still. It looked as if the feet were gripping the ground.

When the creature reached the bank, once again, he very deliberately brought his hand to his chest and flung the back of his hand at them while making the loud "WAH" sound again. He stepped backwards and was swallowed by the thick bushes and was gone in an instant.

The instant the creature was in the buses the entire right side of the woods erupted in noise. Thuds, trees breaking, loud noises. She closed her eyes and they both covered their heads as they thought the trees were coming down.

She stayed like that as the noise started to go away. It got quiet and she heard her friend sigh and saw tears running down her face. They both said, "What was that?" She walked several the several steps to where the creature had been standing, both of them saying "We've got to go!" She did notice a cantilever of a rock out over the stream with a pile of dead crawdads on it, and thinking, "We interrupted them."

They went back to the trail 25-30 yards away to make the remaining 30" hike back to camp. She was terrified but her friend was really struggling and horrified. Her friend was having a panic attack, having trouble breathing, and eventually threw up. They both had went to their bathroom in their clothes during the encounter and hadn't realized it.

When they got back to camp her friend said, "Get me off this f___ing mountain!" By now it was dusk so they carried what they could in one trip and left the rest making their way to the car 20" away.

Her friend was hysteric driving off the mountain. At the bottom they had to stop at the ranger station so the rangers would know they were gone and not missing. Her friend burst into the guard shack screaming at the ranger. She sounded delusional and didn't make any sense. He asked if she was ok, and she screamed "NO!" and ran out.

The ranger said, "It sounds like you ran into a bear", to which she told him it wasn't a bear. He said, "We don't have wild men in these woods." To her it sounded ludicrous. Her friend was blowing the car horn so she told the ranger where they had been, that they had left some gear, and she left.

The next day the friends that had went to meet them called and asked if they were ok. He told her that when they got to the campsite everything was tore up. They had raced off the mountain to call because they thought that something had happened to them.

When she got her camping gear back it scared her so bad that she threw it all away. The lantern was shattered. The folding metal table was still latched but was bent and twisted.

Her friend who had been with her wouldn't take her calls, and shortly after they all left for college. Sadly, her friend was never the same.

The witness lived her life there, was successful, raised her children, and never went back to where the encounter happened. When her children were raised, she moved to Philadelphia to open a business with her sister.

Years later, she ran into her friend's brother at the airport, and he wanted to know what had happened on that camping trip as his sister was never the same after that trip. She cried, trying to somehow explain what she had tried to block out all those years but really couldn't get through it.

It's been three years since she saw her friends brother and since that time she has been doing research to learn about what she had experienced. She is certain that she encountered a Bigfoot that day.

IN ADDITION TO THE STORY, I CAN ADD THE FOLLOWING:

The witness is five feet, eleven inches tall, and when the Bigfoot was crouching, it was eye level with her. She estimated that it was eight feet tall. It was very large; nothing on it was small, almost not real. She has never known that type of terror again.

The head was huge, and the shoulders four feet wide, no tapering waist. It moved unnaturally and smoothly, especially backwards.

She didn't notice ears. The hair was dark brown with red in it. The hair was long on the top of the head and around the jawline, but not on the face. It had sideburn hair. The hair was very thick around the back of the neck and shoulders. The hair was a little thinner on the chest and stomach.

The eyes were very dark but not black. Maybe a little yellow around the sclerae.

The nose reminded her of a boxer's nose. It was large and wide; the bridge was flattened.

The nails on the hands were very dark gray with thin black striations on them. It looked similar to a human hand but leathery. There was a small amount of hair on the knuckles. The hands were darker than the face.

The mouth was huge with thin lips. It seemed to go from ear to ear.

The two times the creature made the "wah" sound, the mouth opened wide, and with the pink inside the mouth, it had some black spots similar to what some dogs have. The mouth was open a little through the entire encounter. The teeth were large square teeth that were yellow.

When the growl happened and he began to back away, he was sexually erect. Each time he made the "wah" sound, he urinated a little.

The Bigfoot had a prominent, heavy brow, with eyes that set deeply back. The head appeared conical, but he had a lot of hair on his head. The hair set back a little on the forehead.

The face was long, and the cheekbones high.

The witnesses thought that it was a monster. It was years later that she realized it was a Bigfoot that she had seen.

FINAL THOUGHTS: I've taken hundreds of reports, and this one was the scariest I had ever heard. I wonder if I could have handled the encounter any better. I was in the woods the next day after taking this report, and I can assure you that I was paying even more attention than normal. She had never told the story to her children and has told just a couple of people other than me. Telling the story caused night terrors and the inability to sleep for a couple of days. It was a real trauma for her and clearly for her best friend, who never recovered from it. She cried throughout the two hours of telling me the story. She reached out to me after hearing my *Wide-Open Research* podcast. I believe her. The Cherokee National Forest continues to be active to this day.

MAN ENCOUNTERS BIGFOOT OVER A FIVE-YEAR PERIOD

LOCATION: Summers County, West Virginia, Route 7, just north of New River on Meadow creek
DATE: 7/3/1974- October 1979

OBSERVED: For 5 years a group of 6-8 men/women aged late teens to early 20s drove from Pennsylvania and went tent camping at the location for 3-4 days. The first year was over the 4th of July weekend of 1974. Each subsequent year, due to work the trip got bumped back a little later, and the last year they went, 1979, it was in October.

While not in a campground, the area was flattened out where others had camped there as well. Frank, the witness, 17 at the time of the first camping trip, had taken some food and walked up the creek a couple of hundred yards to get some alone time.

He was sitting on a large rock that was just a few feet above the creek below. He heard movement and assumed it was a deer, squirrel, whatever, when he saw a small Bigfoot coming down the creek toward him.

At first he thought it was a person, but quickly realized that it was a Bigfoot. It was around four feet tall with dark reddish hair that was almost black. While not muscular, the Bigfoot was stocky for its height. The face was black with no hair around the eyes, nose, or mouth. The nose was human-like but wide and flattened. The hands were gorilla-like, meaning no hair, dark hands, and dark nail beds. The hair was around 6 inches long and more like hair than fur. While the hair didn't look that thick, he couldn't see the skin through the hair.

It walked upright and similar to a human. The eyes were all dark with no white showing. The feet had hair on the top of them. The forehead was flat and small and the head went up to a conical shape. The back of the head didn't have a protuberance showing but the back muscles seemed to go went straight up to the head. The hair was wispy like a horse main and looked a little dirty. He never smelled anything from a distance but later when closer he noticed a wet, moldy smell.

It seemed like the Bigfoot was caught off guard and nervous that he was there. Through the first encounter, and the others, the juvenile Bigfoot would keep looking back and up the other hillside. Frank's impression was maybe for permission or security. The witness could see another animal up there, apparently watching, but could never get a good look at it.

Frank wasn't sure what to do because if it was like a bear and he ran, would it chase him? He slowly laid his food on the rock and backed away. The Bigfoot slowly came forward, took the fruit, and walked back up the creek. The witness stepped forward to watch it until it was too far away to see.

After the encounter, when he went back to camp the others could tell something had happened and began to quiz him. When he finally told them, some thought it must have been a bear. He offered to take the others back then, and over the years, but each time he took anyone else the Bigfoot wouldn't be there, his friends never believed him.

When he went back, he would find berries, acorns, or crabapples laying on the rock many times. He would go each day that he was there and always in the evening. During the day the group of friends would hike and play near what is now the New River Gorge National Park and in the area down the creek from where they had camped.

Over the course of five years he watched the Bigfoot's body change until he was sure it was a female due to breasts. The last year when he saw her, he was initially afraid because of how large she had gotten. She was then about 6 feet tall but had the same color of hair. She was much more muscular, and her hands were large. The hair was thicker than when she was younger. The one on the hill above was still there.

She was never aggressive at any time. The first encounter was quick by the end they may have lasted 15-20 minutes. She always came and went the same way. He would talk to her, kind of baby talk, and the only noise she made was a kind of "coo" like a dove. He always left red apples. At times he left part of a sandwich, but she never took it. One time she took a banana but wasn't sure about it. The next visit he took the banana and peeled it, and she took that. After a few visits she would come closer to him, but he was nervous that she might grab and hold him because of how large her hands were. Her teeth were similar to human teeth.

The campers never heard any noises or sounds that seemed abnormal or out of place in the years they were camped at the location. They did hear scurrying overnight at the camp many times but that could have been any animal.

Frank, the witness, is now a 64-year-old truck driver. The experience never soured him on the woods and while he no longer hunts he did for many years. His truck route is many times at dark and in areas with a history of Bigfoot sightings, but he never had another encounter on his job or while in the woods. Like so many witnesses he thinks about the encounter often.

OVERALL THOUGHTS: We don't have an abundance of reports with the Bigfoot in close proximity of the witness, or lasting more than a few fleeting seconds. We also don't have many reports of witnesses seeing the same Bigfoot over a number of years. It gives us a look at behavior, some of which is expected and others new.

In this case it means the Bigfoot were in the same general area over the years and during different months. As time goes on, it seems as though Bigfoot may stay in the same general area more than we once believed. I see this in a great number of reports, including this older one.

This report gives us a rough idea of what the same Bigfoot may evolve to look like over a period of several years. There are many supposed cases of proclaimed habituation across the country but a scarcity of evidence from the same witnesses. This case may support habituation and/or gifting. We must strive to accumulate evidence from these situations or it's just another story that only Bigfooters believe.

I've said in the past that many people have had Bigfoot encounters while not realizing it because the sounds and behaviors of Bigfoot aren't well known to the general public. If a person doesn't see the Bigfoot, they may not have any idea that they are around.

The area where this report comes from looks largely as it did fifty years ago. If you are familiar with the "halibut effect," Bigfoot are often seen in areas they have been seen historically if the area largely looks the same. In fact, the area of this report is the newest national park in the United States. Bigfoot reports are common in this area, and there are about fifteen reports documented nearby. The *Finding Bigfoot* television show did an episode just seven miles downstream of the encounters.

I received this report from a witness who emailed Cliff Barackman of *Finding Bigfoot* and the North American Bigfoot Center. I spoke to the witness for an hour and a half and exchanged many messages. Later Brad Kennan and I had Frank on our *Wide Open Research* podcast. I've been in the area often and find the witness and location both sincere and believable.

CAMPERS HEAR ACTIVITY AND SHARE TRACKS WITH RANGERS

YEAR: 2016
MONTH: July
LOCATION: West Branch State Park (Ohio)

OBSERVED: Four friends went camping at West Branch State Park. They chose a location in the campground that was near the water and isolated from other camping spots. They had been camping there before and had two tents.

During the night while sitting around the fire they heard things but there were literally dozens of raccoons running everywhere. They also saw eye shine but didn't think much of it because of all the animals running around.

About 3:00 AM she awoke with a sense of dread and a weird feeling. She heard a branch snap but that was after she was awake and laying there quietly. She felt the need to leave and the hair on back of neck was standing up. They left the location.

The next morning they came back and looked around and found large human like footprints, 50-100 of them 50 feet from the tents that were not there the night before. They went and got the rangers. The rangers said it must weigh 400 pounds, but were very reserved. They were supposed to stay another night but left.

OVERALL THOUGHTS: I spoke to this witness at length and found her believable and compelling. I included it because the tracks were verified by the rangers, and she took great pictures that I could include with the report. If you look at a satellite map of the area, you can see that clearly there is not enough room for a Bigfoot to stay there; it was moving through. We only control our land during the day, and who knows what moves through at night. Landowners who put game cameras out near their house are always surprised by what comes by close to their house. While the south and eastern portion of the state of Ohio has some really large tracts of land, I wouldn't call any of it wilderness. I believe that the broken-up tracts and a relatively large population of humans driving around through it account for the great number of Bigfoot sightings. I also think it's interesting that not only does Ohio have a lot of water, but its water runs both north toward the Great Lakes but also south to the Ohio River.

BFRO REPORT #29124
YEAR: 1969
SEASON: Fall
MONTH: November
DATE: 11/24
STATE: West Virginia
COUNTY: Pocahontas
NEAREST TOWN: Marlinton

OBSERVED: It was November,1969, and I was on my first hunting trip with my Winchester 30-30 I had received on my 11th birthday in August. My dad and I were near Marlinton, West Virginia, at a camp site we frequented a lot. I do know the name of the people that owned the land; I will not give it out here even though I know they are deceased.

It was well past daybreak on a clear, crisp morning. (Dad was not one to rise too early since he knew we were hunting on private land with an apple orchard to boot.) so about 7:30 AM we headed out. Now, I could not get to the place now, and Daddy passed away in 1990, but I can draw you maps, layouts, whatever you like because this place was my favorite, and even after this took place, we went there for several years afterwards. As we left the camp house down the dirt road past a small pasture area, you come upon a wooden fence around a hay field that stretched from the dirt road to the river. That river is famous, in my mind, trout river in West Virginia. It was 300 yards from the fence by the road to the fence by the river.

Right at the corner of the fence dad made me kneel down, saying that he had saw a bear. Dad slowly rises and peers through the scope mounted on his 30-06. After what seemed like a decade to me, about 15 seconds, he kneels back down. I said did you lose him, and he said no, it's still there. I said, are you going to shoot him, and he said no because he didn't know what it is. Now my daddy taught me about every critter that ran through the woods, and for him to say that he didn't know what it was, sent me into a shock. He told me to look at it. I always carry field glasses with me when I hunt, I still do.

I slowly stood up, located the animal, and put the glasses to my eyes. I am retired military, and what humans do to humans scares me more than what I saw that morning. It was a very large animal about 9-foot-tall standing across the hay field by the other fence post. There was very little hair on the face, and I remember that he looked like the very kind and wise black man that my father knew. I was not afraid at all, and at the time I thought it was more afraid of us.

I looked at that animal for nearly a minute before kneeling back down. It had brown hair with streaks of red, with a dark brown face, and very dark eyes, but not "without soul." It's hair, not fur, did not seem to be matted or nasty. No, I did not smell anything.

After a minute, Dad and I stood back up and the thing was still there. Dad scoped it, and I glassed it for about 30 seconds when dad said come on, let's head back to camp. Once there, he took my gun and chambered the only round I had in it, then filled the magazine. He loaded a 12 gauge with slugs, then got out a 300 H&R Magnum from the gun case and loaded it. On a beautiful fall day, he would not let me out.

The following morning, a Sunday, you could not hunt till noon. After breakfast, Dad asked what I saw. I told him and he said me too. He said that we should keep it to ourselves, and as far as I know we did. I did share this with my sons after daddy passed away, saying it was the only time I saw him "nervous."

CONDITIONS: Sunny and clear, cool

LANDSCAPE: Hay field, small pastures, hardwood, and apple trees on the hillsides.

FOLLOW-UP INVESTIGATION BY DR. RUSS JONES: I talked to the witness at length about the sighting that his father and he had. The witness is now a fifty-two-year-old retired Air Force veteran. At present he is an operator for an oil field terminal in North Carolina.

His father at the time of the incident was a captain in a fire department near Charleston, West Virginia. His father was also an admiral in the Cherry River Navy, which is a respected informal civic organization founded in 1937 that has included state politicians such as Arch Moore and Robert C. Byrd and national figures such as Dwight Eisenhower and Babe Ruth. He relates that his father was a big, strong man, and this is the only time in his life he saw him panic. In fact, the next day, his father stood on the porch with his .30-06, watching for safety's sake as he went to the outhouse. It should be noted that at no time did the witness feel threatened by the animal.

In addition to what the witness reported, I can also add that they were hunting near the Greenbrier River. The corner of the pasture where the animal was located was overlooking the river. There was also a small apple orchard in the immediate area, which had a lot of deer. This is commonly where they hunted.

When they were walking toward the pasture, they noted the roughly seventy-five head of Angus cattle were stirred up and staying in a ravine near their cabin. They had never seen the cattle in that location before.

The total length of the sighting was five to ten minutes. Based on the height of the fence posts, the witness believed the animal to be around nine feet tall. He also noted that the head was conical in nature.

The family went back to the location many times over the years, and while they had no other sightings, they did hear some noises and sounds that they couldn't readily explain.

As with many witnesses, this witness says that he thinks of that day often. Sometimes a certain morning or setting will serve as a reminder.

One of the reasons that I like this report is that it is a prime example of what the BFRO and many researchers call the "halibut effect." The halibut effect being the belief that if something, whether an animal or a fish, has been found in a certain area, if that area stays about the same environmentally, it would still be a good place to go look for that animal or fish in the future. Although the sighting took place a long time ago, it took place at a location that is still a prime location for Bigfoot sightings in the present.

Regarding the recurring thoughts of the encounter by witnesses, it happens frequently. One witness who drew a sketch for me told me that he had made hundreds of the sketches and thinks of his sighting each day. Having a sighting or even an experience is a life-changing event, I always tell a witness how lucky they were to get to have a sighting, but many don't feel that way, as it may have been scary or traumatizing at that time. I had one witness move from the country to the city in hopes of avoiding another encounter. She apparently suffered post-traumatic stress from her encounter. In reality, most of the encounters don't involve the creature doing anything intimidating or threatening, but apparently it was so unexpected that it forced the witness to once again reevaluate those past and core beliefs they had about such things as nature and the outdoors.

BEHIND THE SCENES: I have told many people that if they could talk and visit witnesses with me, they would have little doubt about the authenticity, not only of the witnesses, but also of the sighting. This witness left me with a compelling story that made it hard for me to sleep after talking to him the first time. What an awesome description that really could only be told from a youth's point of view. While adults can be compelling and interesting, many times youth can describe something in a way that gives more life to a subject.

I wonder if at the end of his life, the father would have talked about the encounter. I have heard and talked to many individuals who have been avid outdoorsman who became very troubled after a sighting, as they were forced to shift their beliefs and understanding of the outdoors. I surmise that this may be the reason why it's so very hard for academics to look at the possibility of a Bigfoot, as it would cause a similar shift in their attitudes and beliefs. Let's be clear that many of them have had negative attitudes and made flippant comments regarding the subject of Bigfoot. No one likes the taste of crow.

BFRO REPORT #38547
YEAR: 1961
SEASON: Summer
MONTH: June
STATE: West Virginia
COUNTY: Wayne
NEAREST TOWN: Huntington
NEAREST ROAD: 8th Street Road

OBSERVED: I'm a 65-year-old physician living in Ocala, Florida. I grew up in Huntington, West Virginia. When I was 14 years old, I was with my best friend Bill Roberts, also 14 years old, and we were walking in the woods behind my grandparent's dairy farm. We had a .22 rifle with us and started roaming around for about an hour when we came to a clearing at the top of the hill.

We suddenly saw an animal that neither of us recognized. When we first saw it, it was bent over doing something with its upper extremities. We were mesmerized for several minutes and did not move. It seemed to become aware of us. What happened next really freaked us out. It stood up on its back legs and looked right at us. We were terrified. It was very tall blackish colored hair, also skinny in its appearance with a tapered face.

It was standing at the edge of a pine thicket. It turned away from us and jumped over a barbed wire fence. Even though we had a gun we ran as fast as we could back to the house to relay the story to my grandfather. I know this description is somewhat different than what you've probably heard, but we saw an animal that I have never seen before or since. S***** P**** M.D.

LANDSCAPE: Pine Forest

FOLLOW-UP INVESTIGATION BY BFRO INVESTIGATOR DR. RUSS JONES: I have communicated a number of times with this physician living in Florida. Although the report is older, it's still important in terms of historical perspective. We have received several reports from this area and county, and this older sighting reinforces the BFRO's belief in the "halibut effect."

In addition to what the witness has in the report, he also added that it was a "frightening experience." Not because the animal was threatening in any way, but that it was an unknown animal that was seen. Without any question, it was tall, black, and bipedal. To this day he will not enter the woods without being armed.

I have met dozens of witnesses, and it's very common to hear that the sighting was often a life-altering experience during their lifetime.

Another interesting point to be noted, Bigfoot is a species, so they are all ages and sizes, from young to old. They don't all look exactly alike.

BEHIND THE STORY: Imagine a story so affected your life that you felt the need to go back fifty years later and file a report just to tell your story. I can't imagine a medical doctor in Florida doesn't have better things to do than file a Bigfoot report and talk about it several times to someone in another state. Witnesses and lifestyles, occupations, and outdoor experiences thereof transcend all occupations, education levels, and socioeconomic levels. Quite frankly, the people who have the Bigfoot sighting may come from any station in life and may or may not have ever heard of Bigfoot before. It's about the location they were at and not necessarily who they are beyond if they are in the outdoors.

BFRO REPORT # 34043
YEAR: 2007
SEASON: Winter
MONTH: November
DAY: Day before Thanksgiving
STATE: West Virginia
COUNTY: Fayette
NEAREST TOWN: Fayetteville
NEAREST ROAD: Route 19

OBSERVED: To keep it short, I was deer hunting in the New River Gorge in Fayetteville, West Virginia, and it was 2007, the week of Thanksgiving. It was evening with two hours of daylight left and I noticed movement about 60 yards towards the gorge from my position. I raised the gun to view the movement through my scope. After holding it in position for 10 seconds or so I saw a very large hand appear from the side of a very large poplar tree. It had its palm facing the tree, so I saw fingers mostly.

Then to my surprise I saw a head peek from around the large tree and two large eyes affixed on a head of a creature I've never seen before and I'm a hunter and have been since I was 8 and now, I'm 38. The Bigfoot blinked twice while looking at me and then stepped back behind the tree. I viewed it for about 20 seconds while it as looking at me.

My mind just couldn't figure out what it was, and I knew what it wasn't. I had no desire to shoot it and very well could have but my mind and body almost seemed to be in a state of shock while viewing it. I had to cross near the location on the trail out of the woos and I was f'n terrified even with a loaded deer rifle. My hair stood on end when I realized that I would have to go toward the location to get out of the woods.

I called my uncle as soon as I got to my jeep and told him, and he believed me. I am a very honest man and would never lie about this. The thing is, though, I never heard it run away or move through the leaves and you can hear movement 200+ yards off in these woods. It's just like it disappeared. I came home very shaken from my experience, and it changed my life now that I know it is out there.

It was very cool looking...about 7 feet tall, it had very large dark pupils and around the pupils the eyes were almost owl like. It had brownish blond fur, and it had a visible face. It almost looked like one of those troll faces that you used to put on your pencils as kids, really, but it was very clean looking and not what you would expect. Its fingers were long and thick with no fur, and it had dark fingernails. I had my scope on power 9 and it was equivalent to being about 30 feet from me visually. It was real and I would take a polygraph and swear on my life.

LANDSCAPE: Top of the river gorge in mixed mesophytic forest.

FOLLOW-UP INVESTIGATION BY BFRO INVESTIGATOR DR. RUSS JONES: I interviewed the witness, who has multiple degrees from WVU. He is a thirty-nine-year-old avid outdoorsman. I hiked to the area of the sighting and was able to see the New River Gorge Bridge close by. One thing I found interesting was the power line right-of-way literally at the location of the sighting. It is believed that Bigfoot will often use rights-of-way as paths to avoid humans and be able to travel long distances in a straight line. In addition, rights-of-way create a natural edge, which is a prime area for wildlife to congregate and feed. The gorge itself is very steep and tough terrain. Maybe some of the steepest in the United States.

BEHIND THE STORY: I introduced the witness to the *Finding Bigfoot* television show, and he was in one of the West Virginia episodes. He was bright, well spoken, educated, and an avid hunter. Who wouldn't be in shock if they had the same experience?

The author has heard wood knocks a couple of different times from the cliffs in the back of the photo. From the clifftop the whole area and a river can be watched

Over the years I have spent thousands of hours in the woods of the New River Gorge. While all of West Virginia is beautiful, many of the places are as diverse as can be. The gorge with its steep canyon walls and cliffs and a world-class whitewater river at the bottom makes the fifty or so miles inaccessible in many places. In certain places there are only gaps in the cliffs every so often to be able to get down to the bottom. There are hundreds of hidden waterfalls, and the rhododendrons and other underbrush can be impenetrable. I have been in places where it may take an hour of scrambling over boulders and climbing under bushes, where you know a lot of snakes are around, to cover a quarter mile.

CONCLUSION
WHERE DOES BIGFOOTING GO FROM HERE?

TECHNOLOGY AND FRUSTRATION

Bigfoot has never been more popular. Part of it, I guess, is the fact that most people's earliest "encounters" with Bigfoot, like mine, relate to the Patterson-Gimlin film, *The Legend of Boggy Creek*, or *In Search Of*. Bigfoot was the monster that the baby boomers grew up with. Have a press conference about a possible dead Bigfoot like a hoaxer did a few years ago and watch over a hundred journalists from all over the world show up.

Technology is improving and getting much cheaper. A thermal just a few years ago cost $10,000, and now a nice unit with recording capability can be had for around $4,000. Flir, the giant company in thermal imagery, is offering cheaper selections and finally has competition such as Pulsar. Although not a body, if enough quality images come in from good sources, and in masses, with other evidence from the same place, like hair samples and footprint casts, it might be scientifically compelling. Game cameras may get quicker and quieter; maybe we will get lucky that way.

I like the idea of using game cameras set to fire at a certain amount of time in intervals in a location that Bigfoot may pass through. It's a lottery, but it's another tool in the toolbox. Of course, it's probably just going to work during the day, with special lenses to see at a distance. If you see something at a distance, there's software to be able to get a better perspective. How loud the camera is wouldn't matter as much because in all likelihood the Bigfoot may not approach right at the camera and wouldn't see it or hear it. If you have a place like that, it might be worth a shot. Good luck with that, but we need to think outside the box and push the envelope.

Maybe someone will develop a way to record with our night-vision gear that is easy and handy. Some of the Gen 3 white phosphorus units are remarkable. Night vision is just not as popular in the field because we can't record, and it still costs around $6,000 for a quality unit. Ideally you would be able to get two people in the field together with both a thermal and night vision.

No question there is more evidence out there, or maybe a greater understanding of the evidence we have. The greatest body of the scientists are still not compelled by what we have, and the truth is that many wouldn't be compelled without a body to eat with their crow. My experience has been that if you can get a scientist alone and talk about what is out there and educate them a little, many are interested. The problem is after getting a scientist interested, gathering additional new evidence is a slow process, so they may lose interest. For, as anyone who spends time in the woods looking for sights, sounds, and evidence of Bigfoot will tell you, more often than not, they don't hear or see anything most of the times we are in the woods.

When I came into the BFRO, it was about three years before I had something happen to me in the woods that I couldn't explain by natural means. Think about that, I'm getting the freshest and hottest reports and going on expeditions and still found action hard to come by. My standard to convince me of Bigfoot activity in the woods is much higher than most of the people I see in the woods. A whistle is probably a bird; a splash in the water is probably a beaver or a fish hitting rather than a rock being thrown by an unacknowledged primate. I have seen few stick structures that I find compelling. A scuff in the dirt is literally anything and probably not a footprint. As the saying goes, "Absence of evidence is not evidence of absence."

The more time that you are in the woods, the greater your chance of experiencing something maybe related to Bigfoot that you can't explain. I would guess most people, like hunters and hikers, don't spend more than a week or two in the woods. Very few of them get very far from a road or trail unless they are riding a four-wheeler, which, of course, can be heard a mile away. I don't know the percentage of people out there who actually go to a remote location that is away from roads and trails, but my guess is it is a tiny fraction.

I try to get out into the woods twice a week year-round. It's easier in West Virginia than in many other places, as wilderness can be just a few moments away in many cases, even in Charleston. One of the frustrations of researchers are armchair academics and skeptics. Certain of these people have strong opinions about Bigfoot and Bigfoot behavior but spend little or no time in the woods. I, being a doctor, understand that many people, of course, have health care issues and aren't able to be in the woods.

If you are not out there, then nothing can happen. Once again, most times, nothing happens that can't be explained through the behavior of common animals. But once in a while, something does happen, and every so often, a bunch of things happen during the same outing! I remember one weekend a group of investigators were out and got "bluff charged," had rocks thrown at them, had a possible sighting, and a camper shaken as they were sleeping. But that is the exception rather than the rule. Years later, we still talk about the weekends where something really exciting happens.

THE FUTURE ROLE OF THE BFRO

How do I think that the BFRO will look in the future? While I think it will continue to evolve, I have no doubt the organization will be at the forefront of Bigfoot research. The members in general are exceptionally passionate, most doing something Bigfoot related each day. A lot of professionals are in the group, so there is greater access to helpful, expensive technology because they have disposable income and access to laboratory equipment and techniques.

The toys cost a lot of money, and many times professionals have the means to put toward hobbies like Bigfoot. Plus, BFRO investigators have access to all reports in the database. They are seeing many reports, public and private, and see the most recent activity and trends and thus have a better chance at being in the right place at the right time, with the right equipment.

Matt Moneymaker is an innovator. I would be surprised if Matt doesn't have another television show in the future. Sure, there are a lot of sharp people out there and a couple of great groups, and I hope they all come up with great ideas to help push research and recognition along. Frankly, I hope they get the evidence that can't be denied. Matt has a lot of detractors, but quite frankly, everyone throws rocks at whoever is on top.

I think it's funny how many detractors Matt Moneymaker has, both on the internet and in books. By and large, many of the active researchers out there got their start by doing a BFRO expedition, filing a report there, or having actually been an investigator for the group. Even his detractors use his database while they spew venom. When one reads articles and forums across the internet, notice they are filled with words developed and used by the BFRO, "Squatch" and "woo" immediately come to mind. Does Matt want to be the first researcher to really come up with something big? Yeah, he and everyone else. I'm sure that Matt has regrets like all of us. Too many people take themselves too seriously.

WHAT IF BIGFOOT EXISTS?

Can you imagine turning on the news and it's being reported that "Believe it or not, Bigfoot is real!" What would it change? Would it be affirmation of all the time we spend in the woods, in front of a microphone, and on the phone? Does it matter? Is it possible that it could happen in West Virginia? Maybe a coal truck takes out one of our barefoot friends? After the dozens looking at one through the scope, does one finally pull the trigger and end the mystery?

Well, certainly history and science books would have to change in an instant. Is Bigfoot some type of missing link or a link? Maybe we find out that Bigfoot is a long-lost ape or an unknown ape. Bigfoot proving to be real may make scientists take a look at some of the other controversial subjects in nature and anthropology with a new seriousness and a more open mind. In an instant we would have scientists with advanced degrees specializing in Bigfoot, and millions and millions of dollars will go into research.

I don't believe that Bigfoot needs us to exist. If Bigfoot has gotten by so far on his own, I hate to see the misguided efforts by uninformed and inefficient but well-intentioned agencies try to create laws to protect Bigfoot's existence or territory. If real, he has existed alongside, literally in some cases, humans for thousands of years. I think it's a romantic and novel idea that Bigfoot is out there existing in the dark, hidden corners of our forests. Its presence out there would show there are things left to be discovered and that man doesn't know everything there is to know about our planet. Maybe in some way we simply need the enigma of Bigfoot to exist as ever-evolving *Homo sapiens*.

Illustration by Sybilla Irwin showing one of my witnesses Bigfoot encounter. Another person who if he chose could have shot a Bigfoot

MY FINAL THOUGHTS

When doing field research, at the very worst you go camping in some of the most beautiful places in the country while seeing many of your best friends and making new ones. You are unplugging from the stressful, hectic rigors of the modern world and getting back to nature the way it was intended. Reconnecting with oneself through nature is both a physical and psychological way to better health, which you can't put a price on. So let's get out there and enjoy all that's out there, all that God has given us.

In the end, the hunt goes on. Do we have more knowledge and evidence than we did five years ago? Yeah, I think so. I really believe that something could break at any time. My friend Monongahela and I have talked about when or how things may break, and he reminded me we thought it may happen twelve years ago! Is it a landowner protecting his animals, a hunter, or maybe a coal truck hits one?

I have relayed a lot of my personal beliefs in this book, many well founded, others not so well founded. I have shared things that are really only known or talked about in the inner circles of Bigfoot researchers. I have done this hoping to show that we all need to work together, share theories, help others as we can. Now doing this second edition seven years later, I can assure the public that we are still not doing this.

TO THE NONBELIEVER

My only hope is that I have given you enough information to make you curious. Enough information for you to think, "There is a chance for something to be out there, even if it's a small one." Enough information that you believe responsible people should really look at the subject seriously. Enough information for you to pause and think, "What if?"

THE APPENDIXES

Included here is the information that didn't fit into the main text, but I think may be important to know, especially for aspiring Bigfooters. It really blows me away how many people are interested in learning more about Bigfoot, the quest, and how to get involved. I reply to many such questions each week.

The first appendix contains old newspaper reports from the history of West Virginia and the immediate southern Ohio border. In summary, Bigfoot-like beings were seen not only many hundreds of years ago by the Native Americans but also reported by pioneers in more recent times.

The second appendix is a listing of websites that I have found useful over the years.

The third concerns the Hewkin-Sullivan guideline, which provides a clear level of expectation in fieldwork.

The final appendix is about the role of the BFRO expeditions in the future "hunt" for Bigfoot.

But first, a short note not sizable enough to make an appendix.

REGARDING SNAKES

It's generally safe to say that if it's 50 degrees or above, it's possible to see a snake. In West Virginia your only worries are the timber rattler and copperhead. Rattlesnakes are shy and will generally warn you while you are a safe distance away, but if you are bitten, you need to seek medical care immediately.

Copperheads are grouchy and cantankerous. They will strike at anything sometimes. While it's a good idea to get medical care, you probably will not die, but could lose a digit. In West Virginia the only recorded people to die of snakebites have been serpent-handling preachers of primitive Pentecostal-type churches. The last preacher to die was 2012.

Most people are not crazy about snakes, but we can't let them keep us out of the woods. I have had them crawl across my boots. And when climbing rocky crags, I have had them lift up right in my face. I'm sure it's a way to make sure your heart is fit!

Should you encounter a snake, slowly back away from the snake, and don't forget my grandpa's old saying about copperheads, "see one, see two," so watch out for the other one!

APPENDIX 1
WILD MEN AND GIANTS

No matter what country you are in, what culture you are talking about or researching, there is always a history of wild men and giants. So I believe when addressing the Bigfoot phenomena, it makes sense to look at the history of wild men and giants in a particular region, as I have found that many of these stories sound remarkably alike and may well be Bigfoot stories. Therefore, it follows that since our barefoot friends are big and wild, they are omnipresent in our region's folklore from the hills, hollows, and history.

Also, I think it's very interesting that in the olden and pioneer times, while these stories are novel and rare, they were still accepted by the populace as generally true. This acceptance indicates that in the frontier era, wild men were assumed real, living in the shadows alongside pioneers and settlers. Whereas today, wild men stories are generally greeted with harsh skepticism. So this part of the book briefly deals with the history of wild men in West Virginia and the surrounding areas as reported in newspapers of old.

Chad Arment, in his excellent book *The Historical Bigfoot*, compiled newspaper accounts of wild men from the early 1800s into the 1940s in forty-two states, including West Virginia, and seven Canadian provinces. It is unlikely Arment's achievement will be surpassed, so I, without reservation, recommend his book to students of Bigfoot history.

In it, Arment makes it clear that misidentification of hermits, itinerants, escaped circus gorillas and the like may account for many of the newspaper stories, along with not a few April Fools' tall tales. But, as with sighting investigations of today, some ring true and clear. My conclusions are, as they spread west, frontiersmen and settlers encountered wild men and were as startled by their encounters and as anxious to report them as hikers and hunters today.

The author thanks Mr. Arment for his permission to use these three reports from his book. The fourth is from the author's files.

A GORILLA IN OHIO (1869)

The *Minnesota Weekly Record*, January 23, 1869. From: Arment p. 227, who in turn found the report in Ron Schaffner's Creature Chronicles website 1997–2006.

"Gallipolis is excited over a hairy man who is reported to haunt the woods near that city. He goes naked, is covered with hair, is gigantic in height, and 'his eyes start from their sockets.' A carriage containing a man and daughter, was attacked by him a few days ago. He is said to have bounded at the father, catching him in a grip like a vice, hurling him to the earth, falling on him and endeavoring to bit and scratch like a wild animal.

"The struggle was long and fearful, rolling and wallowing in the deep mud, (the man) half suffocated, sometimes beneath his adversary, whose burning and maniac eyes glared into his own with murderous and savage intensity. Just as he was about to become exhausted from his exertions, his daughter, taking courage at the imminent danger of her parent, snatched up a rock and hurling it at the head of her father's would be murderer, was fortunate enough to put an end to the struggle by striking him somewhere about the ear. The creature was not stunned, but feeling unequal to further exertion, slowly got up and retired into neighboring copse that skirted the road."

Comment: Gallipolis, in southeast Ohio, lies along the west bank of the Ohio River across from Point Pleasant, West Virginia, in the western foothills of the Appalachian Mountains. Readers should take a few minutes to check the location on Google Earth to better appreciate this report, especially given the year of 1869. Arment also cites four other wild man encounters on the Ohio side of the Ohio River.

Copse is an old term for a grove of trees. Ohio borders West Virginia to the north, and its eastern and southern portions are considered Appalachia. Ohio is renowned for Bigfoot sightings and is presently the number four state in sighting reports. Only the Pacific Northwest has more. All known mammals swim back and forth across the Ohio River.

A WILD MAN (1895)

This One Not of Borneo, but of West Virginia Bluefield, W. Va., Nov. 9. "A party of hunters who were roaming the woods on Elkhorn saw a man ascending a rocky height completely naked. The hunters surrounded the fellow and made an attempt to capture him, but as soon as he saw the men he yelled and ran to the top of the hill."

From the files of the author: *Newark Daily Advocate*, Newark, Ohio, Saturday, November 9, 1895.

Comment: Elkhorn, WV, is in south central West Virginia about fifteen miles northwest of Bluefield. Bluefield lies tight against the Virginia state boundary near the East River Mountain Tunnel. A look on Google Earth confirms this area remains wild, forested, mountain country.

Many people believe that Bigfoot traverse the long mountain ridges in this area and in fact follow the Appalachian Trail, which runs right through the area. The Appalachian Trail is a 2,190-mile-long hiking trail running from Georgia to Maine. It passes through fourteen states, eight national forests, six national parks, and many state parks along the way. It was in planning since the 1920s but was not finished until the 1940s.

MONKEY BUSINESS (1925)

Buckhannon, West Virginia: "The report last week that a wild man was roaming in the country near the Wesleyan camp proved to be an exciting subject for the footballers; but when a party was suggested to be formed including some of the squad, to capture the ape, Coach Russ put an end to the monkey business."

Charleston, West Virginia: *Gazette*, September 6, 1925

Comment: Buckhannon is deep in the mountain forest at roughly the center of West Virginia. Its population today is around 5,700 people, and it is the only incorporated town in Upshur County. Buckhannon is also the home of Wesleyan College. The author surmises there can be no reasonable link made between the student body, the then wildly popular Tarzan of the Apes book series, and a wild ape report at the beginning of the college year.

BLUE DEVIL STILL EVADES TRAPS, WEBSTER GUNS (1939)

Webster Springs, Dec. 8 (AP): "the hunt continues for Webster County's famed 'horse-faced blue devil,' but scores of hunters admitted today that they had not located the mysterious animal 'with a yell like a banshee.'

"Last physical report of any sign of the 'blue devil' came from Mrs. V. S. Cutlip of Diana, who said she heard 'a wild inhuman scream' near her home.

"But residents of the Diana-Grassy creek section, where the 'blue devil.' But that he is too smart to be caught in the scores of bear traps that has been set for him and knows enough to stay hidden when he sees a high-powered rifle. One of the several groups of hunters searching for the beast plans to trap it alive, if possible. In the meantime, credulous folk in the sparsely settled Webster section are very careful about going out at night without a lantern and a gun."

Charleston, West Virginia, *Daily Mail*, December 8, 1939: from Arment page 330.

Comment: Diana, in Webster County, is in east central West

Virginia. This rugged mountainous part of the state remains mostly unsettled.

Arment's book also includes two newspaper accounts of the "blue devil," dated Dec. 13, 1939, and Dec. 24, 1939. Arment is of the opinion that the "blue devil" is not Bigfoot. Indeed, one newspaper article ascribes the beast as a gigantic mole not known to science, and is unlikely to make vocalizations or be caught in a bear trap.

Finally, in regard to this report, note that cougars, bobcats, foxes, and fishers all make inhuman screams as found in the Cornell University Macaulay natural history library previously cited.

APPENDIX 2
EVERYTHING AT YOUR FINGERTIPS

BFRO.NET

This is the go-to website for Bigfooters. With the largest database of Bigfoot reports, the BFRO has investigators who personally vet each report. The site has a wealth of information and keeps abreast of recent developments. The site also shows the public expeditions each year and where they are going to be located.

BIGFOOTENCOUNTERS.COM

An extensive, high-quality site that was put up by the late Bobbie Short (1936–2013). Reports, personality profiles, analyses, and commentary are both well done and informatory. Unfortunately, the site is now largely of historical interest, as it has not been updated since Bobbie's passing.

NORTHAMERCIANBIGFOOTCENTER.COM

The official site of the Bigfoot Museum in Boring, Oregon. Operated by my good friend Cliff Barackman. Full of nice swag and tons of updates on Bigfoot activity. I'm a Patreon member and love his video content.

CLIFFBARACKMAN.COM

Cliff's personal site has field investigations and footprint casts and explanations. As well as sound recordings. It even has a place to report a sighting, and Cliff is kind enough to send quite a few my way! It's easy to spend some time on the site and lose a couple of hours.

THEBIGFOOTDOC.COM

I have to mention my own site as a way to get ahold of whatever books I'm working on or to file a report.

KENTUCKYBIGFOOT.COM

This site is run by Charlie Raymond. It is centered in Kentucky but has a lot of information applicable anywhere. Charlie is a nice guy, a good friend, and very knowledgeable. His expeditions are some of the best around.

SASQUATCHBIOACOUSTIC.BLOGSPOT.COM

This website is the project of the BFRO investigator who helps with many of the audio recordings across the country. He works in the defense industry and therefore uses his pseudonym Monongahela. He is intelligent and has a background in the military. The site will teach you how to build long-duration recorders that can record in the woods for a long time. You can also listen to what are believed to be many of the Bigfoot vocalizations.

SYBILLAIRWIN.COM

Sybilla is the artist for witness sketches involving the BFRO as well as many other Bigfoot witnesses. She is very talented and thoughtful, and it comes through in her work and her interactions with witnesses. It's worth a trip to check her stuff out. I have some of her work in my office; others are in this book! She really is at the very top of the field.

THOMASSTEENBURG.COM

I like Mr. Steenburg. He is an old-school investigator, and I mean that in a good way. He is no-nonsense and has spent a lot of time in the woods with a lot of the Bigfoot legends. There are a lot of archives worth looking at the bottom of the page. Most of the rest is links to podcasts.

PODCASTS THAT I LISTEN TO

Wide Open Research: Of course, this is the one Brad Kennan and I do, so I would really appreciate it if you listen. We have witnesses that no one else has access to as well as the big names in Bigfoot.

Sasquatch Chronicles: Probably close to one thousand episodes that Wes Germer has done, and I'm a big fan. Sure, some aren't that great, but many are awesome, and in totality it's a great way to learn Bigfoot behavior.

Astonishing Legends: If for nothing else than the deep-dive, multipart episodes on the Patterson-Gimlin film.

Sasquatch Tracks: These guys are great with thought-out questions. They have not been doing as many episodes lately.

Bigfoot and Beyond: The legends Cliff and Bobo are fun and interview the who's who in the Bigfoot world.

Apes Among Us: They are from the North American Wood Ape Conservancy. They don't do a lot of episodes, but I respect them, and they are as good as anyone in the business.

Untold Radio AM: Doug Hajicek of MonsterQuest fame is a legend in Bigfoot. Doug always thinks outside the box, and I call him often to get ideas.

The Bigfoot influencers: Tim and Dana Halloran do a fun show with well-known and interesting researchers.

Pine Island Research: Jeff Harding is a hard working investigator and podcaster. He has really interesting stories.

APPENDIX 3

THE HEWKIN-SULLIVAN GUIDELINE

I have found that although I spend hours and hours in the woods each week, I seldom come across Bigfoot evidence. Don't get me wrong, I love and value my time in the remote woods, but most of that time, that's exactly what it is, time in the woods. In the course of a whole year, there are very few actual Bigfoot experiences. Once again, I'm talking about daytime in the woods.

It is a daunting task just trying to get in the same general area as a Bigfoot, let alone come up with some tangible evidence. The frustration of coming up with evidence is the primary reason researchers and scientists leave the field. I have seen dozens and dozens of witnesses get excited and jump in to research after having an encounter, only to be gone shortly because it's hard to come up with much.

In the beginning the "new" researcher is hungry for all things Bigfoot, but the complexities of life, family, and the reality of how challenging the task is can be a deal breaker. When I first heard of the Hewkin-Sullivan guideline, it not only gave me hope and solace, but when I really looked back, I found it, in general terms, to be pretty accurate.

The Hewkin-Sullivan guideline states that for every two hundred hours of actual time spent in the woods in a likely area, you might find one bit of evidence attributable to a Bigfoot such as a footprint, nest, kill, or maybe even a glimpse of one. Now, of course, this might not be applicable in a case of habituation, or some of the "sloppy" evidence so apparent on the internet like a scuff in the ground labeled as a "footprint" or a broken branch called a "tree break."

The creators of the Hewkin-Sullivan guideline were Jim Hewkin and Jack Sullivan. Hewkin was a state of Oregon wildlife biologist active from the mid-'50s into the 1990s. Hewkin's associate Jack Sullivan was a science teacher. For almost forty years they were pioneers in the Bigfoot field in the Pacific Northwest, specifically in the Oregon Coastal and Cascade Mountains. They spent many years in remote Oregon wilderness and set the guideline for others as well as setting realistic expectations for themselves.

My friend Joe Beelart related to me that Hewkin told him that it takes a minimum of ten years to establish a rudimentary Bigfoot database. Interestingly, Hewkin also said that while he and Sullivan always carried cameras and had about a dozen brief sightings or glimpses, they were never able to get a good photograph.

While I have always kept this in mind and been a fan, as time has gone on and I have concentrated my research in a few areas instead of a million, the guideline time has been reduced by about 50%.

PAREIDOLIA

This is also a good time for me to talk about "pareidolia." If you look across the internet, you will see pictures that people have taken believing there is a Bigfoot in them. In many cases people are out walking around, actually just snapping pictures because they have become convinced that Bigfoot is around them in the woods.

Pareidolia is the psychological phenomenon where people look at natural structures and see other things, sometimes things they are looking for, like Bigfoot, or other times seeing things they haven't been looking for, like Bigfoot. But generally, pareidolia is seeing an imagined pattern where one doesn't exist, similar to looking up in the clouds and picking things out in the clouds that look like other objects.

Since this book first came out, and the second edition, along with woo, pareidolia has proliferated as well. With the advent of social media, any given day you can find many examples of people doing this. In some cases maybe they have actually filmed or taken a picture of something but not in the great majority of the cases.

APPENDIX 4
AN INTRODUCTION TO BFRO EXPEDITIONS

This book was designed to inform and excite Bigfoot enthusiasts. At this point, the logical question for those who like to camp and are interested in Bigfoot is where and how to go afield for a search. This is not a new question. Many people, especially in the Pacific Northwest, have developed their own patterns for research. But virtually immediate access to good areas is not available to most people in the USA. Another approach was needed, especially to serve people living in large metropolitan areas who can fly or drive to other parts of the country.

So for over almost two decades, the Bigfoot Field Researchers Organization has led expeditions into likely Bigfoot habitation zones. In those potential habitation zones, expedition leaders and experts provide instruction and practical applications in the search for Bigfoot. This appendix is a short introduction to that process, a process that has evolved and improved over the years. Please keep in mind that expeditions are led by different people, and every one of us does it differently.

THE BFRO WEBSITE

The BFRO website provides detailed information about the expedition location, leaders, type of vehicle required, whether trailers are allowed, and many other specifics necessary to plan a successful outing. The end of this appendix lists some of the practical planning considerations. But most importantly, it is important to schedule vacations and register early. We are pleased to say that most expeditions are filled to capacity well before the jump-off date.

WHAT TO EXPECT

First, an expedition member must allow time to arrive at the campsite. You arrive on Thursday. For those who are not familiar with driving on remote roads, plan on half or less of usual highway speeds. Pay attention on remote roads, not the scenery. If you want to see a view, stop and look; don't drive and look. Road hazards are often encountered, so pay attention to driving conditions. Remember, if there is an accident, first responder help may be hours away.

Expeditions require physical exertion. Sadly, only people who can walk and are in reasonable shape are allowed on them. This is purely for safety purposes. We always ask prospective participants about their health and fitness level, and I have found that everyone is generally too optimistic and generous about their own. Keep in mind that you will be up way into the night, and some will stay up all night. I have found that by Saturday night most people are exhausted. A good walking stick or a set of trekking poles is strongly recommended. Come prepared for the elements since it is rare that an expedition is based at a lodge. Bring sunscreen and a hat.

Plan your foodstuffs so you eat a little all day long. Do not plan on eating two big meals a day. Bring more water than you think you will use. Generally, sometime during the expedition there is a communal meal. If your expedition leader is planning one, think tasty treats, and watch them disappear faster than a Bigfoot in headlights. Some of the expeditions I have led, we fed everyone at each dinner, which is an undertaking. Many other expedition leaders are leading expeditions in remote locations, and you are responsible for bringing your own food. It had evolved to more of a concierge Bigfoot service, so to speak, over the years. I may have largely been responsible for this, starting with the largest expedition ever hosted. I have been reconsidering this, and I believe that moving forward, if I were to lead many more, they will be more of a primitive experience to get deeper into Bigfoot territory. Generally, leaders will try to find a location with some type of store within thirty minutes or so, but it may be a small convenience-type store. Maybe you will get lucky and have a restaurant around. I think that it's reasonable to expect that in Ohio or similar states, but not as likely in more remote states.

There will be instructional classes. Casting prints is almost always on the agenda. If you have a particular outdoor skill, or a set of experiences or knowledge you would like to share, please let your leader know.

Bring a red headlamp and extra batteries. Flashlights are ok to have but only in case of an emergency or around camp (at a minimum because many times Bigfoot will approach camp). Most expeditions will have night walks, which begin well after dark and last into the early a.m. For safety purposes, most of the time you will find yourself in a small group. It is always best to try to walk silently without artificial light, but most of the time this is not possible, especially for inexperienced people. It's a challenge to avoid roots and rocks on a trail when you are tired and only using a red light.

I would expect there to be night vision and thermals present at the expedition. For many people, learning to use and using night vision and thermals will open a whole new world. Another good thing to bring, if already in your kit, is audio recording equipment. Often, it's quite amazing the noises that will happen when people are asleep, or awake for that matter. Many times, there will be audio instruction at the expedition. As previously noted, noises you record are fun to compare to those found around the internet.

Expeditions are a safe, organized way to meet friends for life

EXPEDITION BOILERPLATE...THE RULES

Most of the following rules are obligatory. Also, these are not all the rules, but the main ones. While they may seem restrictive and numerous, most have been adopted from experience.

1. With few exceptions, a minimum age of twenty-one.
2. A participant must have email, access to a computer, and voicemail.
3. No pets of any type regardless of the circumstances.
4. No guns, period.
5. No cancellations due to weather. Marine Corps air-conditioning rules apply. Come prepared for expected high and low temperatures and precipitation.
6. As previously noted, expedition fees vary and are nonrefundable. If there is an exceptional circumstance, you may receive a credit toward another expedition.
7. No alcohol.
8. You are going to sign a waiver of liability and that you won't tell others where you went.

Doing an expedition is a labor of love, love of the subject and group. Incapable people are not put in charge of expeditions. You will get to meet some of the very best researchers around.

Did the Native Americans sometimes call Bigfoot the "Stone man" because he hid among the rocks, walked the rocky ridges, or threw rocks? Whose to say, maybe all of them

BIBLIOGRAPHY
BOOKS ABOUT BIGFOOT I LOVE AND RECOMMEND

Arment, Chad: *The Historical Bigfoot*. Landsville, PA: Coachwhip Books. This book is an outstanding compilation of old newspaper accounts about wild men in the United States and Canada. The introductory chapters provide excellent commentary on what is, in some cases, a cultural phenomenon.

Coleman, Loren: *Bigfoot! The True Story of Apes in America*. New York: Paraview Pocket Books, 2003. Loren is the king of cryptozoology books. He keeps a pulse on what is going on in the entire cryptozoological field and regularly speaks on the subject.

Green, John: *Sasquatch: The Apes Among Us*. Surry, BC, 1978, and Hancock House 2006. Mr. Green is one of the true legends in Bigfoot history. A journalist by trade, Mr. Green was the first to interview many widespread witnesses at his own expense. He was also the first to publish a major compilation of their stories. Mr. Green's work remains relevant today, as the title was republished in 2006.

Krantz, Dr. Grover S.: *Bigfoot Sasquatch Evidence*. Hancock House, 1999. This was the first widely circulated book on the subject written by a scientist. As such, it is important to read from a science perspective. I have reread this book often.

Meldrum, Dr. D. Jeffery: *Sasquatch: Legend meets Science*. Forge Books, 2006. Dr. Meldrum is a tenured university professor whom the press often reaches to as the scientist in the know regarding Bigfoot. Dr. Meldrum is the expert on Bigfoot track casts.

Murphy, Christopher L.: *Know the Sasquatch*. Hancock House, 2010. This book is a must read for Bigfoot enthusiasts. It is filled with historic photographs and interviews with Bigfoot greats no longer with us.

Powell, Thom: *The Locals*. Hancock House, 2003. Powell is a science teacher, longtime field researcher, and former BFRO curator. A great read with great stories. It's just as relevant as when Thom wrote it.

MORE RECENTLY PUBLISHED

Beelart, Joe, and Olson, Cliff: *The Oregon Bigfoot Highway*. Williamette City Press, 2015. The authors provide a very thorough look at one of the most active Bigfoot regions in the United States. I found a wealth of information in this book that I hadn't previously considered.

Powell, Thom: *Edges of Science*. Williamette City Press, 2015. Thom's second nonfiction book is a great accompaniment to his first. I have always admired his writing style and found it readable. Thom always makes me think outside the box with his progressive takes. I am not as quick to dismiss ideas that are paranormal after reading his books.

Jones, Russell: *The Appalachian Bigfoot*. Into the Fray Publishing, 2021. This is my second book. It was number one on Amazon for seventeen weeks and covers my theories, thoughts, and hypotheses on Bigfoot as well as the best Bigfoot stories in the Appalachian region.

Halloran, Tim: The Bigfoot Influencers. Hangar 1 Publishing, 2022. Interviews with the people on cutting edge of Bigfoot or contributing to Bigfoot.

ACKNOWLEDGMENTS

My thanks to the following people of which without none of this would have happened. Some have provided me insight, others guidance, some love and support. It's hard to share a life with someone so consumed to a subject like Bigfoot. Imagine listening to him talk about it 20 hours a week, do a podcast, spend part of a couple of days in the woods a week, it's a lot. My people humble me. Thank you.

Linda Andresen
Pete Andresen
Kevin Osborne
Scott Morris
Matt Moneymaker
Cliff Barackman
G. Michael Hopf
Tahnee Hopf
And not lastly, Shawnda and Makena 🤍

ABOUT THE AUTHOR

Dr. Russ Jones has been in private practice for over 30 years and consumed with the Bigfoot phenomenon for far longer. He just completed a second edition of his award winning first book *Tracking*

the Stone Man. His Second book *The Appalachian Bigfoot,* was number one on Amazon for 17 weeks.

After attending Huntington College on a baseball scholarship, he graduated from Palmer College of Chiropractic. He has a BS degree and Doctor degrees.

Dr. Jones is also a Certified Master Naturalist. He attempts to mix a science background with a lifetime of hunting and trapping knowledge to gather possible evidence of an undiscovered North American primate.

He enters the woods with his faithful black lab "Shade" to tend his dozens of professional game cameras and look for tracks year round in Appalachia.

 twitter.com/Bigfoot_doc
instagram.com/Bigfootdoc

ALSO BY DR. RUSSELL JONES

The Appalachian Bigfoot

Made in United States
North Haven, CT
09 May 2023

36446698R00152